MY TRANSITIONS

BOOK COVERS: GIFT FROM MICKEY AND BOB KNOX

NANCY K. SCHLOSSBERG

the Peppertree Press
www.peppertreepublishing.com

Richard Olin

Dedication

I dedicate this to Richard Olin, my significant other, who kept urging me to write it for my children and grandchildren, and who gives joy and meaning to this last part of my life; to Ellen Hoffman, my longtime editor whose last email before she died stressed how important it was to tell my life as a series of transitions connected to my transition theory; to Barbara Peters Smith, a friend and talented writer and editor, who helped me turn lots of text and talk into a manageable narrative – and who felt the book could be of value to others as they struggle to figure out how to cope with transitions; and to Mickey and Bob Knox who surprised me with the cover picture of my books.

Barbara Peters Smith

Bob and Mickey Knox and
Nancy and Steve Schlossberg

TABLE OF CONTENTS

Foreword

Robert Frost famously wrote, "Good fences make good neighbors." I would like to add: And so does random chance. I became the author's across-the-hall neighbor when my husband and I moved into a senior living condominium, aka "a retirement community." Had we not been proximate to each other, I doubt we would have become such good friends.

We actually had much in common. Both of us were only children raised in privileged circumstances. Both of us were writers: she as an academician, I as a newspaperwoman. Though manifestly dissimilar in purpose and execution, we were both advice givers. After being a syndicated opinion columnist, I was the first "Dear Prudence" at *Slate*. Nancy's advice, of course, was not dispensed in newspapers ... but in classrooms, textbooks, and lecture halls. She made her name and reputation as the go-to person on the subject of transitions. All kinds of transitions. In no way was her area of expertise narrow, transitions being both varied and unavoidable in people's lives. If one were to try to create a headline for her life's work, it probably would be, "How To Live Life."

The beauty part of Nancy's work is that she developed "Transition Theory." It is not easy in the Academy to plow new ground, but that is what she did. Her full professorship at the University of Maryland was Ground Zero for her work.

Although supposedly retired ... she's not really. There was, I would say, a Renaissance when she was 90! There were invitations to Zoom into meetings in Australia, requests from national reporters who were writing about transitions of many kinds, and speaking invitations. She had made the field of "transitions" her own.

And I will tell you, as the neighbor from across the hall, that Nancy – at 94 – is one of the best-looking, best dressed women in the building. She is sharp and funny … and her own transition to this point has been brilliant.

Margo Howard
Sarasota, December 2022

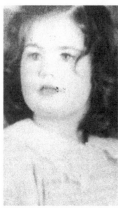
Nancy as a baby

Early 40's

Now

Introduction

IN MY DREAM I was on the Appalachian Trail, a place I had never thought of going or even wanting to go. But there I was, struggling to follow the path. Suddenly, I needed a bathroom. I started looking frantically but could not find one. I became scared. What should I do?

I left the trail to continue looking. As I kept getting farther away from the trail, I began wondering if I would ever find my way back. Finally, with a force of will I turned around. Exhausted, I found the trail again.

That dream was the main thing I remember from my two weeks at the Sarasota Memorial Hospital with breakthrough Covid and pneumonia at the age of 92. That dream occurred during the time the doctors kept telling my son they expected me to die. I thought of the dream as my metaphor for struggling to live in a frightening situation.

As I was waking from the dream I was in a haze, thinking, "I have to live for my three grandchildren, Robin, Jenny and Stevie. I also have to live for Richard." He was a neighbor, recently widowed, and he and I were in a new relationship. I remember dreaming or thinking, *I don't want him to have to go through another death so soon.*

My health has returned; I am back to myself. But having faced the real possibility of death prompts me to reflect on my life. I, like everyone else, have had a life of transitions – some expected, many that came as a surprise, and others that were expected but did not occur. Over the years, my personal and professional lives merged. As I was living through transitions, I was also developing a transition theory that enabled me to understand what I was going through, how to manage it and move on. Clearly transitions are my brand.

This memoir is not a survival story. It is a story of someone who was destined to live a traditional life as mother and wife. Instead I carved another life, a non-traditional path full of many transitions and surprises. This book will cover my story with selected pictures, a few of the columns I wrote about different transition issues, and a summary of transition theory.

I hope my reflections on my life will provide a framework for others to examine their own lives, and find strategies to cope in situations that can sometimes feel like a loss of direction.

PART I

My Story

Chapter One

Reaching Adulthood through Trial and Error

AS AN ONLY CHILD, I grew up feeling loved and attended to. In many ways I had a happy childhood – lots of friends, and close double cousins with whom I spent summers. But life was not without trauma. My mother lost a baby when I was four, and that changed her forever. That broke her heart and I believe her alcoholism was the result.

My first memory was waiting at the door of our home for my parents to return with the new baby. I saw them walking up the driveway, my father holding my mother to give her support. It was a breech baby and the doctors did not know how to save her. She was the sister I never had.

Nancy and her mother

By the time I was an adolescent, with the crowd coming over to listen to music and hang out on Saturday nights, I realized my mother was an alcoholic. She only drank after 5 p.m. but the martinis would affect her. I hated the change in how she talked.

She was overly involved with me, which was embarrassing. But at the same time, she was my biggest supporter – adoring me, providing opportunities like entering me in a community theater at age 12, taking me horseback riding, ice skating, going on painting field trips and, of course, shopping sprees.

My feelings about my mother were ambivalent. While I was scared when she drank, I both loved and admired her. She could play the piano beautifully. I especially remember "Red Sails in the Sunset."

But at the same time, I was so ashamed of her. I could not talk about it with even my best friend, Marcia. I was in constant conflict, both loving and hating my mother's actions after 5 p.m. when she would start drinking. So, I suffered, and when I went away to college an ulcer was discovered. It disappeared when I graduated from college, and never reappeared.

I remember one night when Mother chased me around the kitchen with a knife. She didn't realize what she was doing. Thank heavens for Maggie, our wonderful housekeeper who was my protector. She took Mother upstairs and came and comforted me when I went to bed. I am still grateful to her for that, and for the many ways she cared for me.

I had boyfriends in high school; the most meaningful was Wally Bonn. He was kind to me and realized what was going on with my mother. We did not discuss it, but I knew he was there for me. Years later, I met Wally and his wife and had a chance to thank him for being my support in junior and senior high school. In those days we necked, but did not sleep with boys.

If my mother had been less volatile I might have stayed in Pittsburgh. This way, I eventually moved away and developed my own identity. The wonderful thing about living longer: I began to understand the cause of her alcoholism and to forgive her. I became free to remember her with love and appreciation for all the things she had done for me.

I adored my father but it was not until I was an adult that we became very close. He was charismatic, and in Abraham Maslow's terms a fully actualized person. After graduating from Wharton College, he went to work for his father, a builder. After several years he realized he could not work with his father. He left but they maintained a close relationship. He then opened a Chevrolet car dealership. He retired at 50 and became a stockbroker. But most important he was a community leader, heading up the community chest and taking a leadership role in any group. I loved being with him but really did not get to know him well until I was an adult, after my mother died in her 70s. My father lived until his late 80s.

Eventually he became attached to a woman. They did not live together but traveled and saw each other almost every night. My husband and I did not like her. She was selfish, arrogant and spoiled. However, when my father asked me what I "really" thought of her, I decided not to rain on his parade. So, I said, "I am thrilled for you, that you have a relationship with someone; you enjoy life traveling, dancing and being together." I later urged him to increase what he was going to leave her in his will. After he died, I never saw her again – but always felt good that I did not cause trouble for him.

To summarize my family life: As an only child I was listened to and appreciated. I think that gave me confidence to speak out, and as an adult I was comfortable making speeches. I was clearly an extrovert, following in my parents' footsteps.

But my identity is not that of an only child. I was never lonely; I had a great group of friends. We had an amazing crowd of boys and girls – always doing something together. And then there were my double cousins. I spent summers with them on Long Island and remember playing Monopoly, going to Jones beach and other fun things. I was also close to my Uncle Harry who taught me to tell time and my grandfather (my father's father) and my grandmother (my mother's mother).

Here's how I came to have double cousins: My mother Gertrude Robin and Dotty Kamin had been best friends in college. Dotty introduced my mother to her brother Saul Kamin, and my mother introduced

The Double Cousins – Nancy, Joyce, Albert and Cynthia

her brother, Nat Robin, to Dotty. The two couples married, and my parents are my cousins' aunt and uncle, and their parents are my aunt and uncle. All our other relatives – grandparents, and so on – were what we had in common.

There were three double cousins: Cynthia the oldest, then Albert and Joyce. I was very close to Cynthia growing up; we were born a few months apart. After Cynthia married and moved to Puerto Rico I saw less of her and more of Joyce. Unfortunately. Joyce got cancer and died; then Albert died. After that, Cynthia and I renewed our relationship. She had been so much a part of my growing up.

Cynthia died a few months ago, in Puerto Rico. Her adult children have been very supportive. Over the years I have become close to Robin, her daughter, and spent time with Chris, one of her sons. I loved Jeff, who died, and have enjoyed talking to Michael and Andy.

My grandmother on my mother's side lived in New York City. She taught me chess at age 12 and later when I was a student at Barnard College in New York City we spent lots of time together. She was very liberal and progressive, worrying my parents that she might influence me – which of course she did. Although I never met my grandfather Robin, he had a great influence on me, as a pioneering medical doctor widely known for his altruism.

Pittsburgh friends

Nancy, Judy, Donald, Lois, Wally and his wife, Norma Sue

My four years in college were my unhappiest years. I felt very insecure, and upset with my parents. I was very conflicted about my mother: I couldn't wait to get away but at the same time I was very dependent.

The decision to attend Barnard was a practical one. It was 1947, and getting into college was hard for females. Our high school guidance counselor would not support a Jewish girl submitting too many applications. We took this for granted; it was not upsetting at that time. My mother had graduated from Barnard, which gave me extra points.

I had been an A student in high school but was a C+/B- student in college. As I look back, I would have been happier at a school like Antioch, where work was an important component of learning. If you had told me then that I would have a successful life, both in terms of family and career, that I would even write books or become an academic, I would not have believed you. I was so far from that. I wasn't a star; I was just an attractive girl from Pittsburgh who was popular with boys and girls.

One summer during college, I went to Europe on a steamer. On the way back I met Charles Van Doren, a very handsome English instructor at Columbia, and another passenger David Boroff, who was a rough guy and not at all middle-class. Charles was the son of the poet Mark Van Doren, and in 1959 would become famous – and then notorious – as a television quiz show contestant. Of course, I picked David, and when my parents met the boat they couldn't believe I had let Charles get away. Years later, I couldn't wait to call my mother when he got all that publicity for cheating on the TV quiz show.

By this time, I felt like everybody at Barnard except me had lost her virginity. My grandmother's apartment is where I lost mine with David Boroff. What was I thinking? I suppose it was like a rebellious thing. And do you know what he said to me? "You have a beautiful back."

I had three significant relationships in college. First, I met my oldest, dearest friend, Janet McKee, on the first day of school. She was grounded and sure of herself; I was not sure of myself.

Janet's parents ran a farm in Massachusetts for people who had no financial resources and needed to be in a protective environment. I came from a well-to-do Jewish family. But we bonded and understood each other. Janet is the person who later introduced me to Steve, and she was the go-to person for my children. I trusted Janet and admired her. She had a full life, but now is in a California assisted-living facility near one of her sons Tim. We talk occasionally on the phone. I love her sons, Michael, Chris, Tim and her daughter-in-law Marie. I keep in touch with Tim and occasionally with Chris and Marie. They were like family to me. I miss Janet.

My other two significant college relationships were with the main men I dated, Stanley Ostrow and Mike Cohen. They were both in law school – Stanley at Yale and Mike at Columbia. Stanley planned to live in Pittsburgh; Mike planned to live in New York City. I picked Mike and married him in 1951 right after graduation. I was very attracted to Stanley, but did not want to live in Pittsburgh.

If I married Stan, I imagined, he would come home from work and ask about the children; I would have an apron on, getting dinner. I knew even then, before Betty Friedan, that I did not want a traditional marriage.

My mother had worked at Carnegie Tech in the drama department, but she left her job when I was born. That struck me as ridiculous. Here was a talented woman who gave up her career to raise me. I always thought she would have handled her life better if she had stayed at work. But in the 1930s that was, for the most part, not done.

Although I never met Barnard's president, Millicent Macintosh, I admired the fact that she was a wife, mother, and college president. I remember thinking, "That is what I want – a life combining work and family."

I was talking recently with friends who graduated from Smith in 1951, the same year I graduated from Barnard. Adlai Stevenson was their commencement speaker, and he congratulated all the Smith grads because now they were prepared for their new roles in life, as wives and community leaders.

I suppose I married right after graduating because it was the expected thing, and the decision between my two suitors was not fully conscious. I made the choice to go with my vision of a life free of parents and Pittsburgh, rather than my sexual fantasy. I didn't have the guts to move to New York on my own, and Mike was safe. As I look back, the choice set my path as an independent woman.

After college, marriage and the move to New York, I got fired from my first two jobs. The first was one I was unsuited for, as a file clerk for the National Industrial Labor Board. The next was a store, Bonniers, now closed. It carried sophisticated modern furniture, as well as books on the first floor. Instead of pushing the more popular books, I kept telling people they should read books by authors like Owen Lattimore. My supervisor did not like that.

One day I told my supervisor that it was freezing on the sales floor. She said, "Go tell Mr. Bonnier." I had no idea she was being sarcastic, so I did as she told me. Mr. Bonnier heard me out, and replied, "Then you should dress more warmly."

But the *coup de grace* was when I told her I would be taking Christmas week off because I always went to Pittsburgh to be with my family. I remember calling my father and saying I got fired and he said, "It's time to talk about how to behave in the business world."

These firings turned out to be a formative experience. Years later I was asked to be the keynote speaker at a conference of college student leaders. I told them, "You will leave school and you will think people are still going to listen to your ideas. Be prepared for temporary downward mobility."

After the furniture store fiasco, I asked a placement office to send me on one job that was not secretarial. I was referred to the Tobé-Coburn School for Fashion Careers, where I became director of admissions. It was founded in 1937 by Tobé Coller Davis, a worldwide fashion authority, and Julia Coburn, former fashion editor of the *Ladies Home Journal* and president of the

Fashion Group. Miss Tobé was the fashion person; Miss Coburn operated the school.

One day Miss Coburn said the Gimbels – of the famous department store family – had called; their daughter had just been rejected by our school and they were very upset. I said I had interviewed the daughter, and this was not what she wanted to do. Miss Coburn commented, "You're the best director of admissions we've ever had – but we're wondering why enrollment has gone down."

I realized working for a profit school did not fit with my values. I decided to go to Columbia and take a course in interviewing. That was what led to my pursuing a doctorate.

Mike was supportive when I was getting my degree. I wasn't desperately in love with him to begin with; there was no sexual excitement. He was sexually competent but I wasn't at that time. For a while he was crazy about me; but as I started pulling away so did he.

I remember sitting at Tobé-Coburn and saying to myself that he was a wonderful man and I could be married to him for the rest of my life. If I had gotten pregnant and had children, I would have remained married. We got divorced at my initiation. My 10-year marriage to Mike gave me the support and space to begin to grow up, to become less emotionally tied to my parents, and forge my own career path.

In 1951 I graduated from college and married Mike; in 1961 I received my doctorate from Teachers College at Columbia and divorced Mike. One funny story. I was living alone in a walk-up brownstone on 9th street in the Village. I was eager to finish my doctorate and get on with my life and make some money. I had my final meeting with my advisor. She marked up my dissertation with a red pencil. Those were the days when we typed and mimeographed. I left the meeting with the only copy with final suggested changes. I took a bus to dinner to meet with friends and when I sat down I realized I had left my dissertation on the bus. I was HORRIFIED. I called the bus company but lost and found would not be available until the next day. So, I got a cab and started going around the city stopping every bus on that route asking, "Are you the driver who was whistling A Rose Must Remain?" Finally, one driver said yes. I ran to the back of the bus and there was the one and only copy of

Magnolia Harris my savior

my dissertation. Hurrah! Years later I was given an award from Teachers College, Columbia. Instead of thanking every relative and teacher I ever had I told the dissertation story ending by saying I clearly am in the wrong field. I should have been a detective.

My twenties were important, as it was during that time that I was becoming who I am today.

Chapter Two

A Surprising Love that Defines a Life

MY HUSBAND STEVE SCHLOSSBERG was a remarkable person – charismatic, ugly-handsome, committed to the labor movement and to social justice. He was the one person in my life with whom I have been completely authentic. We said what was on our minds; we told each other how we felt; we shared our vulnerabilities.

He constantly told me how much he loved me. I told him I was going to enroll him in AA to help get over his addiction to me. But of course, I loved how expressive he was. He was a man of passion and purpose.

We had 48 years together. Steve died at age 90. Steve was perfect for me and thought the same about me for him. Yes, we

John, Nancy, Steve, and Janet

had a few big verbal fights, but they were not destructive. We often resolved them with humor.

Steve came into my life at the best possible time. After my first marriage to Mike Cohen ended in 1961, I moved with my miniature Schnauzer to a third-floor walkup in Greenwich Village. I had a good job at Pratt Institute and was dating different men. I had a lot of adventures, and I'm so lucky I did not have children in my 20s. I had been married to a very nice man and had a caring, compassionate divorce.

In 1961 – the year I obtained my doctorate at Teachers College, Columbia University and the year of my divorce to Mike – I went with my friend Florence to Greece and Turkey and what was then Yugoslavia. We were in Dubrovnik at this lovely hotel, and I recognized a man who was the music critic of the Pittsburgh Post-Gazette and a friend of my father's, Donald Steinfirst. He told us his wife Jane was ill in their hotel room, and he invited us to accompany him that night to a performance of *Carmina Burana* in the walled city. We were thrilled – but later that day the manager at the hotel told me, "Mr. Steinfirst wants to see you right away. His wife has just died."

He was beside himself, of course. He said he would not cremate her body, and it turned out that getting a body embalmed and ready to fly home from Dubrovnik was very difficult. Florence and I spent the whole trip visiting cemeteries and interviewing funeral directors. It was very, very complicated, but we were determined to see this through for him.

We heard that the then diplomat and foreign policy expert George F. Kennan was coming to town. When he walked into the airport, I was there with questions about our dilemma. I don't know how we finally managed it, but in the end we arranged to have the body embalmed and shipped to Pittsburgh. Then I received a telegram from my parents: "Don't go to Yugoslavia. Our friend just died in Dubrovnik."

My work at Pratt was another interesting adventure. Esther Lloyd-Jones had been my academic advisor in graduate school at Columbia and was also on the board at Pratt. That was probably how I got the job as dean of freshmen. The students there were highly creative and unconventional, even before the '60s got fully underway. One day Esther told me, "The board doesn't like the way students are going out in the community looking for apartments: please tell them how to dress."

The next time one of these students came to my office, I began an uncomfortable discussion about the need to dress more formally, wearing shoes, since he represented the school in the larger community, and the board had concerns about this.

The student responded, "You're telling me how to dress? If we're going to suggest things, let's look at you. You're very good-looking and you have great legs. But you're wearing a green dress with white piping, and you wear your hair like a fur piece." When my secretary in the adjoining office heard this, she laughed so hard she fell off her chair. After that I went to Miss Bergdorf's, got a new hairstyle, and the student and I became great friends.

But Pratt was an unusual place at that time. The president Richard Heindel and his wife lived in a building with a top floor that had been made into a presidential suite. One night, she died after falling down a trash chute into the incinerator. I asked myself, "How do you fall down an incinerator chute? You don't fall; you get pushed." I was thinking that maybe I should leave Pratt – and luckily, it was around then that I met Steve.

I had just broken up with a professor from New York University whom I had met at a professional conference.

Nancy and Steve –
Wedding Day

Actually, he jilted me – saying, "My psychiatrist told me I am not ready to get married." I remembered that Janet, my best friend from college, then living in DC, had once told me that if I did not get back together with my first husband, she knew someone I might like. I was feeling sorry for myself about the breakup, but was not so unhappy that I was unable to dial Janet and arrange to take the train to DC (in those days we had dial phones!).

Moments after I was introduced to Steve Schlossberg, this charismatic, warm, loving man, I fell in love. He was this big guy, the warmest person you've ever seen. He just enveloped you, and he gave me this big hug.

Janet's husband John Silard was one of the great civil rights lawyers, and the two of them arranged this encounter. Janet was very, very New England. Her father was a minister, and her parents ran Gould Farm in Massachusetts, one of the first communities for mentally impaired adults. Janet was the most centered, mature person; she was so self-confident that she was elected class president.

Steve adored Janet – but he didn't want anybody like Janet. He called her a granola bar. So, he claimed he was busy all weekend, but had a few hours free on Friday night. At our introduction I was wearing a fez that I had bought on my trip to eastern Europe with Florence. He was wearing a pipe holder around his belt; it looked so ridiculous that we both started laughing.

I was 32 and he was 40. That first night we laughed, talked and made plans to see each other the next day. I went back to New York hoping I would see him again. Steve was then working for the Federal Mediation Service and was in charge of negotiating the New York newspaper strike. He called when he was in New York, and then invited me to DC for Thanksgiving. I took him home to meet my parents at Christmas. We were engaged, then married in June 1963.

When I moved from New York to DC with Steve, he was already an emerging national figure as mediator of the 1961 newspaper strike. When people asked whom I was dating, I would say, "a national failure," since the strike went on and on. The Secretary of Labor at the time, Willard Wirtz, even called Steve to ask if I was the cause of prolonging the strike.

I trusted Steve from the very first, and I guess he trusted me. He had everything I was looking for: He was charismatic, engaging, attractive, warm and socially committed to changing the world. He was doing important things and he was a man of principle.

He had some faults, too – and we had several enormous fights. He was so passionate about what he believed in. One time, we were at a party. I was in the dining room, and I heard this loud voice from the living room saying, "Fuck the flag!" I had no doubt that this was my husband. For years I would say, when we were on the way to a party, "Don't be yourself."

Then there was a political event in Detroit: One of Hubert Humphrey's advisors Joseph Rauh, a leading civil rights lawyer and partner of John Silard's, was in town for Humphrey's speech. Humphrey was running for president, and some people running the program were undercutting Humphrey. Joe was a guest at our home, and when Steve started yelling at John Conyers for not being positive about Humphrey, I got furious. I left the event by myself, and when they came home I was eating a pint of vanilla ice cream. I agreed with Steve that Conyers was wrong, but did not like the way he expressed his disagreement. We called that one "El Incidente." By the way, Steve and Conyers resumed their friendship a few years later.

When I was hosting a fourth birthday party for my daughter Karen, her little brother Mark, who was two, would not stop biting her. I said to Mark, "If you keep biting Karen, I'm going to bite *you*." Well, he did – and I did. And as I tell him now whenever he brings it up, I'd do it again.

Mark ran inside to Mrs. May, our wonderful housekeeper, and told her that I bit him. He was crying, and Mrs. May started to cry. This was when Steve came home. Meanwhile, I was outside trying to keep the party going. Then Steve came out and shouted, in front of all the mothers, "I'm going to put you in a mental institution!" Again, I did not speak to him for several days.

On a trip to Lake Como in Italy, we were sitting outside at a restaurant, and there were hundreds of pigeons. I didn't know I had a phobia about pigeons. I went and asked if we could have a table inside, and they said no. I started getting panicky and saying I had to go back to the hotel. By the time they brought the food, I was up and running. Steve was trying to pay the check, and calling, "Nancy! Nancy!"

Later that night he said he was going to write a letter to the NM. I asked who the NM was. His answer: "the New Man and I will warn him about you." I told him I was flattered to think I could get a new man, and we started laughing about it. For years, whenever I did something he thought was crazy, he would say, "It's going in the letter."

I adored him. We shared so much trust and such commitment; I don't know how many people have that. What amazed me is that the kids really liked how close the two of us were. They adored their father: He was so inclusive; he was so warm. I knew that he was really interested in my wellbeing. He was not threatened by me in the least and he wanted me to be successful. He was also wise politically as well as a practicing feminist. He really promoted my career while he pursued his own so passionately.

One time I was supposed to speak on television about a women's issue in Detroit. I had a terrible case of laryngitis, and the doctor told me absolutely not to talk. I was determined to go on the air because it was such an important topic, but Steve stood in my way in front of the bedroom door. He kept reminding me what the doctor had said. I was so angry, I just started pounding on his chest. It is the only time either of us ever hit the other.

Then he said, "I know what we'll do. Get me one of your BS articles on women's issues. I will go and speak for you, and you can say a few words at the end." That's what we did.

Steve was very loving and demonstrative about his feelings for me. My friend Gail Levin told me recently that when her husband Richard was dying, he kept telling her how much he loved her. She said to him, "What's happened to you? Do you think you're Steve Schlossberg? "

In the years after Steve died, I have dated other men and actually had two significant relationships. To help me deal with his loss I was fortunate to learn about Paul White, a wonderful therapist in Sarasota. I asked him what was wrong with me; why did I want to be involved with a man?

His answer: "You had such a good relationship with Steve, you wanted more." I know many women are not interested in that. In fact, a friend told me that once her husband died, she was no longer interested "in pots and pans or prostate glands!"

Steve was my mentor, someone who knew me thoroughly and had a gift for guiding me onto the right path. I remember an incident in 1973, 10 years into our marriage. My mother wanted to come down to DC from Pittsburgh for Labor Day weekend. I didn't really want her to come.

Steve said, "Nancy, there are two people in your life who adore you with no reservations. That's me and your mother."

Of course, I urged her to visit. We had a wonderful time shopping at Lord and Taylor buying school clothes for the children who were then seven and five. Right after that visit, my parents went to the Greenbrier resort in West Virginia to celebrate their anniversary and have a full physical checkup. It was there that my mother learned her bladder cancer had spread to her brain.

I realized then that I was so lucky I had listened to Steve. That was the last fun time I had with my mother before a two-year decline that led to her death.

My parents were wonderful grandparents. Two stories. When Karen was 4, I showed her a picture of the new shades I was going to order for her room. They were very contemporary—large pink polka dots. She said "No. I want a room that looks like Grammy's". My mother had traditional furniture. Karen and my mother adored each other. My mother often said if she had known you could love an adopted child as much as a biological one she would have had more children.

One night my father, Mark and I found ourselves alone and decided to go out for dinner. Mark was 10 or 11 and the conversation was going nowhere. To get things rolling, I asked my father to tell Mark stories about his growing up and how he dealt with the difficult times he had in school My father described the terrible advice he received from a teacher that he would never be a success if he did not learn to sit still and behave. My father described how he decided not to let those words come true. And in fact, they did not. He was a successful businessman, father, husband and community leader. At the end of this conversation I asked Mark to respond. His only comment surprised me. "When did you lose your virginity?" Without missing a beat my father responded, "I was not hoping to date the headmaster's daughter like you are trying to do."

My mother and Karen

My charismatic father

Chapter Three

How Detroit Started My Engine

I DIDN'T WANT TO GO TO DETROIT. And in a fascinating way, it might have been the best move I ever made. It was in Detroit that I began to seriously become involved in my career, and grow as a wife and mother.

This was in 1963. I had just married Steve. One day he told me that Walter Reuther, who led the United Auto Workers

Mark, Nancy and Karen

union, wanted to interview him for the role of general counsel. It would mean leaving DC, where I had a job at Howard University that I loved. I resisted the idea of leaving.

Steve said, "Nancy. There is one Walter Reuther, and there are many universities."

When we got to Detroit, Steve had a meeting downtown with his new colleagues. While I waited for him to finish, I noticed a sign for the Detroit Chamber of Commerce. I don't know where I got this idea, but I went inside.

The woman at the desk asked if I needed help, and I said yes. "I need counseling. I have to move here and I don't want to," I said. "Can I talk to someone who can tell me what's good about your city?"

Eventually I ended up in a room with a man who probably was surprised to find himself there. I explained my dilemma, and he started by asking me what I liked about living in DC. I talked about my house and my work and the great views.

And he said, "Well. You live in an urban renewal neighborhood, so you'll live in one here, Lafayette Park, that was designed by Mies van der Rohe. You liked Howard University; you'll like Wayne State. And tonight you should go to this restaurant that is at the top of one of our tallest buildings, so you can look out and discover how beautiful Detroit is."

We did go out to that restaurant. And when I saw Detroit spread out before me, I sobbed all through dinner. In my opinion, it did not compare to D.C.

When I had moved to DC from New York in 1962 to be with Steve, Howard University was the place that had welcomed me with not one, but three job offers. Before that, I interviewed at the Manpower Institute with an acquaintance of Steve's who said, "I would hire you in a minute – but I can't. Cookies like you have babies."

At Howard, they told me I could be the director of admissions or dean of students, but I thought a Black person should be in those jobs at a historically Black university. So I took the post of assistant director of the counseling center, which was a great fit.

At that time, Howard could accept the top third of students from any school. Many students from poor high schools were therefore admitted. After a semester at Howard they flunked out. I remember saying to the staff that we needed a survival support program to help such students. I was shocked when several staff members said, "Well, we made it on our own." That attitude would change in the late 1960s, when white faculty would not be overly respected and students were given more support.

After that experience, Detroit was a shock to my system. We did move into a Mies van der Rohe starter house, but while Steve was wrapped up in his new life, I was at sea. I flunked knitting, then I took up sculpture, which wasn't much better. I was 33 years old and I didn't know what to do with myself. One night when Steve came home from work asking what was new, I told him that nothing was new, and my career was over.

He responded, "Nancy, you've got lots of resources, and you're just whining." I stopped talking to him for two days. But I knew he was right.

I met a social worker, Harold Johnson, who needed a volunteer at the Brewster-Douglass Housing Project. "These kids are not getting any career guidance," he told me. I agreed to help out. We made flyers that said, if you are a junior or a senior in high school and you want to talk about your future, come to this desk.

It was a lot like the volunteer work I had done in the Hell's Kitchen neighborhood of New York when I was finishing up at Columbia. I didn't look like I belonged in Hell's Kitchen, but there had been some murders and the kids needed career counseling. A youth employment program was located in the Hartley House Settlement, and my task was to sit at a desk and help the kids who didn't qualify for those jobs. I remember thinking that if I could get them engaged in an industry they liked, then they could move on from there.

One of the boys loved movies, so I took him to Radio City Music Hall, where he helped the janitor clean up. Another told me he liked guns. I said, "OK." I took out the Yellow Pages and looked up small detective agencies. I found him a job sweeping up the office at one of them. At least this got him close.

The community had a closed-door meeting and decided to offer me a permanent job for $2,000 a year. I had graduated by then and had a job opportunity at Pratt, and I couldn't afford to take their offer – but I was so honored that the community voted to select me.

This volunteer work in Hell's Kitchen and Detroit led me to my whole way of thinking about moving from theory to practice. You have to have a solid theoretical framework, and then you can figure out what to do.

At Brewster-Douglass, I remember a young Black girl who expressed no interest in anything except going to the barber shop with her uncle when he had his hair cut. "That's the one thing I'd love to do," she said – cut hair. I arranged for a barber school to talk to her, and they accepted her into their training program. She became the first female barber in Detroit. Then I identified a place for the student to apply, the Urban League supplied the funding. The mothers at Brewster Douglass also raised money by organizing a dinner. They gave the Urban League representative and me an award. Another honor I treasured.

Shortly after this I saw a profile in the Reporter magazine about Jerry Cavanagh, Detroit's mayor. I decided to write him a letter asking if I could be of help – not realizing that that very day, the city council had decided to make Detroit he first city to get money under President Lyndon Johnson's new poverty program.

It turned out that to launch this new initiative, which the city called TAP – Total Action against Poverty – they basically needed a go-fer with brains. Cavanaugh read my letter and assumed that because I was coming from Howard University, I must be Black. They called me and soon hired me.

I liked Jerry Cavanagh, and it was a fabulous experience. Because Steve was with the UAW, I had access to the political world of Detroit. Soon I was interviewing people all over the city.

The project went well. Detroit was awarded one of the first grants under the program, and I was offered a position to work on the project. At the same time, Wayne University offered me a chance to go back to teaching, although it was not a tenure-track role. Steve said, "Do not take the job in the city; you'll be eaten up alive. The Wayne offer, you'll turn into something – and that can be your career."

When Steve told me to go with Wayne, I went in and filled out an application form which included a health record with a question, "Have you ever had therapy?" I got a call that I needed to come back and answer a question about one of my responses. They wanted to know: Why did I have therapy?

"Do you ask people who have not had therapy why they haven't?" I demanded. I went on: "I'm feeling angry right now, and I don't often get angry. You can look at me and see how I handle anger, and get an idea of my mental health." I was sure I had hurt my chance for a job, but the chair of the counseling department intervened.

Steve and I were enveloped in the social world of the UAW – a community of people who believed in the same things. I wasn't getting anywhere in my career, but I was enjoying myself and learning about the importance of the labor movement.

I happened to mention my lack of academic progress to a colleague, who told me he thought the problem was a woman in the department, who was something of a *grande dame*. He said, "You wear your hair just like she does, with a band; stop wearing your hair that way."

I decided to give up wearing headbands. At the next faculty meeting this woman asked, "Why aren't we putting Nancy up for tenure?"

Through Steve, I met a political historian at Wayne State named Lee Benson. His wife had multiple sclerosis and was pretty incapacitated. One time the four of us got together and they told me that their daughter Sally was leaving soon for college. I said to Eugenia, "Now that Sally's going off to school, what are you going to do with your life?"

There was dead silence. In the car Steve told me he couldn't believe I had asked her such a question.

The next morning, Lee called. He said, "We could not sleep last night; can you come over?" When I did, he told me, "The fact that you asked what she was going to do, like she was able to do things, was mind-blowing."

I helped them figure out a plan. Eugenia had spent a number of years helping returning women plan for their careers. We figured out that she could run groups in her home but this time focus on individuals with disabilities. That sort of thing is what turns me on – making a difference and helping somebody figure out options when none were apparent.

In time I went from being an assistant professor at Wayne to a tenured associate. I worked with Lillian Troll, a Professor at Wayne, and we did one of the first studies on counselor bias, having to do with age. Then John Pietrofessa and I did one of the first studies on gender bias – the kind you wouldn't be allowed to conduct today, because we used actor-clients who were playing a role. When the client was a woman, all the counselors in our study – male and female – pushed her into an educational career path instead of engineering. In fact, our study became a background paper for the President's Commission on the Status of Women and is still quoted in the literature.

Later, when we were just about to move back to DC, I was called to testify about these findings before Sen. Walter Mondale's committee on gender bias. I explained how we used false clients. Someone on the committee joked, "Is that why you had to leave Detroit?"

I learned a great deal at Wayne.; it was how I got into the work that I do now. And also how I learned how to be an activist.

At the same time, I was beginning to foster my intellectual life. My doctoral dissertation at Columbia had been related to adult socialization, and I was very interested in the question: Can adults change? To answer this question, I decided to look at men 35 and older who were enrolled at Wayne State. These had been blue-collar workers who were in the process of changing their lives by pursuing higher education. There were 625 men who fit this demographic, and I wanted to get to know them. I wrote each of them a letter that began, "I have become interested – no, fascinated – with men like you." Of course, I had a huge response.

In speeches later on, I would say that I had contact information on 600 men who thought I was wonderful, and whenever my husband got out of line, I threatened to go to this list and pick one.

One was a janitor becoming a teacher. For all of them, there was a presumption that they had to support the family. My work became focused on studying the assumptions about what it's appropriate for older people to do. These assumptions are person-made; they are not biological, but based on what Bernice Neugarten, a scholar in the field of aging, labeled, "social clocks." I was getting really involved in the issues of adult development – changing, pushing against expectations.

When we were moving back to Washington, there was a well-known professor of social work, Fritz Redl, who was retiring that year. The Wayne State board of governors asked him to speak and asked me to speak too; it was such an honor. I was beginning to get recognized for my work.

Also, before I left Detroit, I got an invitation from the College Board to serve on a commission about testing. I said it sounded interesting, but I had two little children and was working full-time. The board representative said, "Are you telling me that you're busier than the journalist author John Hersey?" I joined the commission, and met many impressive people. The commission met in Sarasota. Little did I imagine that we would later retire there.

Things like that happened early in my career. I didn't really feel I deserved them at that point.

Chapter Four

Striking a New Balance as a Working Mother

Counseling Psychology Colleagues: Roger Myers, Nancy Schlossberg, Jane Goodman, Sunny Hansen and Alen Ivey

WHEN I WAS AN ASSISTANT PROFESSOR at Wayne State University, we had two children; life was busy. One day I announced that I would have to resign from Wayne. I could not run the house, care for two children under three, and prepare for classes.

Steve's response changed my life: "You cannot resign. First of all, you are not good at housekeeping. But more important, if you leave your job you will be a woman in and out of the labor movement with no career. You are someone who should have a career because you have much to offer."At some point Walter Reuther said to Steve, "I don't care how busy Nancy is, you can't bring the children to negations!" And that was in 1966. Amazing.

We found out that we both had fertility issues, and in the 1960s, the treatments were not sophisticated: They brought

41

me in and blew something up inside me. It was so painful, I thought I was going to die.

I said to Steve, "I don't think my genes are so fabulous that I have to give birth; let's look into adoption." But the adoption agencies considered a woman in her 30s too old to be a new mother, and they all wanted me to guarantee that I wouldn't work. Even the man at the Jewish agency insisted that a mother needed to be home with her children. I said to him, "Have you read *Portnoy's Complaint?*"

It appeared that our best hope was a private adoption. There was a judge we knew in Detroit; he and his wife had four or five children they had adopted privately and legally. Our dear friend Jeanne Nunn was the lawyer who handled things for us. She consulted a doctor who knew in advance about Karen being born.

I met Karen when she was less than a week old. Back then, if you adopted privately, the child had to go to a foster home for three weeks while they investigated you. My mother flew in, and we went every day to visit Karen at the foster home.

While I waited, I found a big wooden board and turned it into a collage pasting all kinds of things on it for her room. Then Karen came home and I realized I didn't know how to make baby formula. I called the foster mother, and she and her daughter came over and they taught me.

Two years later, trying to add the second child was more difficult. One lawyer called Steve and said his daughter was having a baby; he asked for money under the table. We knew that wouldn't work. Then we heard from the doctor about Mark.

Jeanne was the most generous person; once again she handled the whole thing. The social worker came to interview me and inspect the home. We were sitting in the kitchen. The social worker said, "So, how is your marriage?" I said. "Well, it's fine except for a few areas. We fight over the thermostat, and I don't like the way he drives."

When she left, Steve asked me, "I can't believe you said that." I said it was the truth! Actually, the social workers for Karen and Mark were both wonderful, because they knew I was working and they didn't give me any trouble about that.

Mark was born during the riots in Detroit. We could hear the guns and mayhem downtown. Karen had been so easy that I assumed that I was a magical mother. Mark was premature, colicky and ugly. He's so handsome now! But I would wheel him around the neighborhood and people would say, "That's a beautiful blanket; did you make it?"

Mark screamed all night, and I couldn't give him any medications because our doctor didn't believe in masking symptoms. Soon I concluded that I was not this magical mother and I needed a baby nurse. We found Myrtle May, who had an eighth-grade education and the wisdom of the ages.

When I called, she told me she had several clients ahead of me, and couldn't even get to where we lived during the riots.

Mrs. Myrtle May

"I'll come as soon as it's not cordoned off," she promised.

Mrs. May appeared, and life changed forever. Every other night she would stay over so I could get some sleep.

When we told her we were moving back to Washington, she broke down. After we moved she would come on her vacation to stay with us for a week every year, and came when Mark had a hernia operation. Mark missed her so much, and would cry, "I want my May."

As parents, we were very *laissez-faire*, very loving and had a lot of fun in our house. But raising children is complicated and sometimes they drive you crazy. They were each wonderful and difficult in different ways, at different periods. Mark's colic sort of upset the family apple cart. When Karen was an adolescent she was testing us. Our house in Maryland had a lot of nooks and crannies, and she spent a good deal of time avoiding us.

One morning when Karen was a senior in high school, we woke up and she announced that she was leaving home. She was going to live with a friend she'd worked with in a bar, and not going to college. This was at 7 in the morning, and we had full days ahead of us. I just said that we'd all meet at home after school and talk about it.

That day I had been invited by a producer at the Maryland Public Broadcasting Corporation to DC to hear the anthropologist Barbara Myerhoff speak. We were working together on videos for a course on adult development, and we thought it would be interesting to have her in one of the films. As I was sitting with the producer, Barbara Myerhoff opened the meeting by talking about the importance of secular rituals.

"For example," she said, "if a 17- or 18-year-old decides to leave home, you could get very angry. Or you could have a ritual that helps with the transition. After all, here is a child trying to become an adult. A ritual will help someone connect who she is – a child – with who she is becoming – a young adult."

I called Steve and said, "Don't yell at Karen tonight. I have a whole new take on it."

Janet and John, our best friends with their three boys, came for dinner to ritualize Karen's decision. Everyone gave her a toast. We gave Karen the money to install a new phone but she would have to pay the monthly phone bills. Thanks to Barbara Myeroff, we never had a fight. Karen moved out, and eventually got a bachelor's and a master's degree. We never had a disruption in our relationship over that.

Later, when Karen and Larry got married, their children were the flower girls. Karen chose to have her wedding at the Woman's National Democratic Club, and it was lovely. John Silard, Janet's husband, played the cello with his granddaughter, Chris Silard performed the marriage ceremony and Steve was able to walk Karen down the aisle. Several years later Mark and Michele married on the beach and Steve was able to participate. Both weddings were beautiful and simple.

A memorable experience with Mark: He was a football player in high school, a quarterback. In the last game of the season, he threw the losing pass. After the game, he seemed a little off. I called a therapist colleague who had been a football player, and he said, "I think you should take him to the hospital; I think he's got a concussion." And he did.

At the end of the year there was a football dinner, and we all went. Everybody on the team got an award but Mark – who was humiliated, especially because his grandfather came to the event.

The next day, Mark skipped school and somehow got himself downtown to his father's office. He told his father his life was over. Steve said, "Let's take a walk." They walked and talked, and later Mark used the experience in his college application essay.

I was at dinner the other night with a group of women, and something came up about a person we knew. One of the women said, "Well, he's adopted" – as if that explained a whole lot. I said, "I don't mean to overreact, but I'm a mother who adopted two children. These are my children; they're my flesh and blood, not literally but figuratively."

It does make me a little defensive because people act like adoption is a second-best alternative. After all, look at all the people who don't do well who aren't adopted. I'm not at all unhappy that I didn't give birth. I never felt cheated. Why are people so proud of their genetic heritage?

Steve and I treated adoption like a non-event. But here's where I was dead wrong: To children, at some point in their lives, it does matter. I was wrong to think of adoption as a non-event, because it's a major event for the children. Someone had rejected them, no matter the reason. It took me a while to treat it like a major event for my children.

When Mark was 10 or 11, we were in Wellfleet, Massachusetts, where we went for the summers. There was a square dance, and Karen was allowed to go because she was two years older. We were sitting on the beach with a group of friends and Mark started with me: "I'm going to the square dance too. You can't boss me; you're not my real mother."

I said something light like, "I think I am; I pay all the bills." But later, in private, I said to Mark, "That kind of talk does not make you look good."

When Mark was about 18, he wanted to find his biological mother. I had always told the kids I would help them with this in any way I could. Once again Jeanne Nunn stepped up. She got in touch with the biological mother, who said she'd been waiting for someone to contact her. She turned out to

Nancy and Jeanne Nunn

be a professor of organizational psychology at one of the California universities.

I was shocked when I got a call from her before they were to talk. Mark's biological father had just died – she wasn't married to him – and she thought I should be the one to tell my son. She and I ended up talking about psychology.

As it turned out, the meeting was unsettling for Mark. She was very needy, and I think it frightened him.

Karen was horrified by Mark's search for his biological mother. She said, "Oh my God; we're going to be on *20/20*, the wonderful blended family, blah blah blah."

I told her, "I'd be curious if I were you. But if you're not, it's your life."

Then, out of the blue, Karen got a letter from the state of Michigan: Her biological mother wanted to see her. The mother lived out West and her daughter, a lawyer, was the one who made the contact.

Karen delayed and delayed. Finally, I asked if I could write to her. I said, "This woman is suffering. She gave birth to you; she wants to know if you're OK. Can you give me permission to write and tell her what a wonderful young woman you are?"

Finally, she said she would talk with them. She agreed to meet, but only if Steve and I were there too. Steve had the idea of a boat trip around D.C. so, we all went for a boat ride together, and then had lunch at Janet's. It turned out that her biological mother was a farmer and an artist – like Karen – who had an affair with an older man when she was young.

I said to Karen, "The more people who love you in this world, the better your life is."

I don't think Steve and I were the best parents in the world, although Mark and Karen are marvelous people and parents. I thought our family dinners were horrible: We had conversations, led by Steve because his life was interesting to them, but all the while they were kicking each other under the table. Of course, they remember these dinners as terrific.

Although balancing motherhood and an academic career was challenging – especially in Detroit when the children were small and when my career required "publish or perish" – I found inspiration from a memory of something I had heard while working at the Pratt Institute in Brooklyn in 1961.

After I got my doctorate I was the dean of freshmen at Pratt, which meant I was in charge of all the residences. The people who ran these dorms were not professionals; they were women from Europe whose husbands had been famous in the arts. I told them, "We are not going to spend our time together talking about toilet paper and toothpaste. We are going to talk about the roles of women."

Mark and Karen

The first speaker I invited to one of these meetings was a professor in the architecture department at Pratt, Sibyl Moholy-Nagy, who had been married to the Hungarian Bauhaus architect Laszlo Moholy-Nagy. Sibyl remarked, "Dr. Cohen has asked me to speak about the role of women, but I'm going to speak about the joys of uncommitted love." I almost fainted when she said that.

I don't remember what she said about the joys of uncommitted love, but I'll never forget her story that changed my life. She had two daughters, and her husband who felt that her role should be that of a wife and mother. But she decided to claim for herself ten minutes alone in the morning. "I had a pad of paper in the bathroom," she told us. "Every morning I wrote for ten minutes, and after five years, I had a book!"

That was a game changer. In Detroit I remembered about Sibyl's ten minutes a day. That led to my waking up every morning before the kids and writing for half an hour. I just was consistent about taking that time. And that gave me a map for my career. I was able to publish refereed journal articles and later books just by being consistent.

Also, I created a way to learn new things. Since I couldn't leave home and go to academic conferences, it occurred to me that I could host my own conferences and have the experts come to me. I met with the provost at Wayne State and asked for funding for the first conference. After that, they became self-supporting. As an aside, all through my academic life at Wayne and Maryland I found great support for my research and conferences. I was a very happy academic.

There were very few scholars at this time studying adult development, and the one I most wanted to meet was Bernice Neugarten. She had written a great deal in this area; I was intrigued by her ideas about "social clocks" – the concept that adults are expected to reach certain stages in their lives, like marriage or owning a home, by a certain deadline. These were not determined by biology but by social norms. I wanted to learn from her.

Bernice lived in Chicago and when I called to invite her to Detroit, she said she was fully booked and couldn't come for two years. I said, "Fine. Give me a date, and I'll arrange everything." Then I went to the provost and asked him to support my conference – which he did.

I gathered a panel of the original group of men I had studied, who attended Wayne State when they were over 35. It was the highlight of the conference as Bernice interacted with them. And that started what would become my annual conferences on adult development.

Later, when the children were older, I was able to attend professional conferences out of town. There was the American Counseling Association, the National Career Development Association – and the main one, the American Psychological Association, which published my last three books.

My professional involvement with these associations was an important part of my life, and I immersed myself in the work with total support from Steve. We had one issue when we had just moved back from Detroit: At our house in Westmoreland Hills, we were standing in our driveway one morning, going in different directions.

I said, "I can't get home until 9 o'clock tonight." Steve said, "I'm testifying today and I can't pick the kids up from school." This prompted us to realize we had to have a live-in housekeeper who drove. Juggling home, children, work and friends was sometimes daunting, but I had amazing resources.

Chapter Five

Speaking Up as a Woman in the Active Voice

WHEN I WAS STILL AT WAYNE STATE, I was continuing hosting my conferences and getting a lot of support. I received a call from the president of the university, asking me to chair a committee to examine women faculty and students in terms of equity. It was one of the first such commissions in the country.

Steve advised me, "You say yes – because you're going to get your eyes opened. Take that assignment so you can learn what women are going through." I followed his advice, as usual; he was wiser than I, and his world was working with Blacks and whites and politics.

One of the eye-opening instances of gender discrimination related to faculty and staff insurance. Although both male and female faculty and staff paid equally into the annuity system, retired women received a smaller monthly payout. The insurance company, TIAA-CREF, defended the practice because according to its actuarial tables, women lived longer than men. In the federal case we brought, *Peters v. Wayne State University*, the court agreed with us that this was a Title IX violation because the uneven payments discriminated against women as individuals. The case received a lot of attention and I was on the news.

I was beginning to be active and have a voice. There was a student at Wayne, Jane Goodman, one of the brightest students I ever had. She wanted to talk about how we could challenge the Strong Occupational Interest Inventory, a career guidance tool that had a tradition of using pink-tinted paper forms for women, and blue ones for men. If a man took the pink form he would be advised to go into nursing; If he took the blue form he would be advised to become a doctor. We petitioned to speak about this at the American Counseling Association's annual meeting. We had considered pursuing the legal route but our husbands, both lawyers, advised against that. I wasn't a public speaker at that point; I was so nervous I kept going to the bathroom as we waited to be heard.

During this period, I was interviewed frequently by local news reporters about my involvement in women's issues. One time, we were watching the evening news, expecting to see me on camera. But while they were talking about Nancy Schlossberg there was a mistake, and what we saw was footage of Miss America coming down a runway. I couldn't believe it; I was furious. But later I saw that it was funny.

I left Wayne in 1972 as a full-blown activist. After TIAA-CREF and Strong, I was much more of an advocate for gender equality.

My passion for activism actually started when I was in high school. There was a contest in the city of Pittsburgh to write an essay about ways to stop juvenile delinquency. I wrote an essay and won a prize: a check for $5 or $10. I saved that check for years.

In Pittsburgh, there was a Jewish sorority, and I was invited to join, even though I was a little young to get in. The nickname was SOP, and most of the major cities had chapters. It was a breeding ground for becoming a Jewish princess. Everything was fine until we had to talk about what happened with the next group to invite in – and I was so appalled. There was one girl in particular; the discussion about her and the decision not to let her in sickened me, and I resigned.

An early inspiration for taking this kind of stand was my grandfather Albert Robin, the one I never met because he died before I was born. I had no idea how they got here from Russia and how he obtained a medical degree, but they ended up in Wilmington, Delaware. My grandfather's story has been a major influence in my life.

The story my mother told me was that one day, Irénée du Pont came into my grandfather's office and offered him a check for $10,000 to thank him for his discovery that the infections in Wilmington were coming from the water supply. Then my grandfather tore up the check and said, "I'm a doctor; that's what I do." Du Pont offered him stock in his company instead, and he said, "I can't accept; I'm a pacifist."

The two men became best friends. He was the only one who knew my grandfather in his 50s had a heart condition. When my grandparent's house burned down, they temporarily moved into the Dupont's home and later gave my parents a beautiful silver tea set as a wedding present – which now sits in Karen's farm amidst the goats and yarn.

This picture of a principled man who was dedicated and was not always thinking about money impressed me.

After his death, my grandmother moved to New York, where she would become my mentor when I attended college. Eva Halpern Robin was an activist in her own right; in 1920, as president of the Delaware Equal Suffrage Association, she led the group in a successful lobbying effort for a special session of the state assembly to consider ratifying the 19th Amendment. After that body adjourned without the desired vote, she worked to unseat the politicians responsible.

Born in Russia in 1878, she came to the United States with her parents in 1883. In the early 1930s she returned twice to what was then the Soviet Union, researching its educational

Nancy speaking

and criminal justice systems with the intention of publishing a book.

During the second world war her hosting of a "Saturday Forum Lunch Group" brought her to the attention of the Congressional Committee on Unamerican Activities. They thought it might be a communist front organization. In 1948 her phone was tapped and an investigator came to see her. In 1953, she railed against McCarthyism. But she told me she was not a card-carrying member of the Communist Party because she thought she could do better without that label.

This was all part of my background.

When we moved back to Washington from Detroit, I saw a position listed in the Chronicle of Higher Education: The American Council on Education (ACE) was seeking its first woman executive, to encourage more women to become college presidents. I was very lucky to get the job; I would be working with all kinds of interesting leaders in higher education.

A lot of impressive people had been considered for this post, and I was honored to be chosen. I had arrived at a place where I could help education productively, assertively. Within three months I was deflated; I had been wrong; I had failed.

Except for the first day on the job when the president asked me to lunch, not one executive invited me to eat with him; almost every day my peers ate at a nearby club. And when I spoke up at our weekly staff meetings, not only were my comments ignored – but often they were not even reflected in the minutes!

At first this embarrassed me, then it depressed me and finally it angered me. I was selected for the post as a leader in the women's movement, because I was noticeable, assertive but not abrasive. The horror was the realization that I could not speak publicly on issues important to me, and at the same time I had no influence in the administrative inner circle. I had become a non-person. I began to feel adolescent and uncomfortable. I felt whiny, complaining, inadequate. I blamed myself for all that was happening.

One day I attended a public meeting at the Office of Education. I said, "I'm now going to speak as an individual," and I talked about my experience with the TIAA-CREF lawsuit. The next day, I heard that the president of TIAA-CREF had flown down to Washington to talk to the President of ACE, Roger Heyns about ACE's woman executive.

I ran into Roger's office and said, "I heard you had a big meeting," and asked why I wasn't included. He said, "You should have been there, but it was last-minute; we arranged it in the men's room."

That incident did it. I became furious at them instead of myself. I realized they could not accept a woman as a co-equal and the problem was theirs. The crucial thing is that I saw the problem as external and real. My depression lifted; my anger mobilized and my *joie de vivre* returned. I was in fact working in a hostile environment, and I could not be part of this establishment.

By the time I got to the University of Maryland, my reputation was not as a scholar, but as an activist for women's issues. The opening was for a visiting professor, but something in me thought, "I'll get on that campus and it will work out." A year later I was a full tenured professor, and I had a wonderful 26 years there. Women were still a small percentage of tenured full professors. I did not realize at the time how unusual my situation was.

I was able to do my research with small faculty grants. I had excellent colleagues and wonderful students. I grew into a full-fledged professional. I was happy even though I heard many faculty members "bitching." I was very productive, but realized that I needed secretarial support. At that time faculty members did not have personal secretaries.

I figured out a way to have the support I needed to continue being productive: I went to Central Administration and suggested a plan where I would have some of my consulting money sent to the university and they, in turn, would hire a part-time secretary for me. Betty Bowers provided the needed support. I used to call her Betty Darling. One day Betty called, asked to speak to Steve, and told him, "If we both leave Nancy the world will find out she is a cipher!" Steve and I couldn't stop laughing. Betty made life easy for me and we worked so well together.

I had lots of good colleagues and friends at Maryland. One, Jan Birk, was really the individual who originally connected me to the department. Jan and I became good colleagues and very close friends. We still have phone visits. She is so solid as a friend, so loyal, so trustworthy. The other, Barbara Finkelstein is still in my life. Barbara and I carpooled together. We

Jan Blrk and Nancy

shared lots of family events as we had children the same age. I admired her intellect and sense of fun. I am still in touch with two former students who became friends and colleagues, Mary Ann Beattie and Stephanie Kay. Stephanie and I started a consulting firm and developed the TransitionGuide, a self-scoring instrument that helps individuals identify their coping resources. After moving to Florida three of us (Susan Komives, Sylvia Rosenfeld and me) would get together for an annual catch up in Sarasota or St. Petersberg.

Early on, I was asked to be on a committee looking at Title IX and women's basketball. There was a push for this committee not to go overboard on spending for women, because men's sports were very important at Maryland. There were a variety of people on the committee: one student, a couple of tenured professors, some administrators. And then there was the head coach of the University. By chance, he and I always sat opposite each other. At one point I teased him by saying, "Coach, don't you think it would be great for us to have a bake sale, so we could raise money for women's basketball?"

Sylvia Rosenfeld, Nancy and Susan Komives

On Valentine's Day people on the committee gave me a big card allegedly signed by the head coach, and after our work was done he actually wrote me a nice note. All along, we had a good time at the meetings. I always try to build fun into what I'm doing, even when it's very serious.

Finally, we came to a meeting where we were supposed to vote on the allocation of funds. I didn't often get calls at home

Barbara Finklestein, Nancy and Steve

from the college president, so I was surprised to hear from him the night before the vote. The next day, there was a new person from the board of governors who had been asked to sit in on our committee. I said, "It's wonderful to have you, but since you don't have the background we can't possibly take the vote today." A week later, when we held a secret ballot, only one person voted against the proposal – and that was me. The student member of the committee told the college newspaper that the opposing vote was his, but it wasn't true. The Washington Post called me for comment, but I said, "I'm not the chair of the committee, and there's no way I can talk to you."

In 1979, I somehow talked the executives at NBC into letting me tape six shows on adult development for their Knowledge Series. At first, they turned the idea down, because it was the international "Year of the Child" – but I kept trying and they said yes. I didn't know a soul there, but I apparently had the ability to persist. Not sure I have the same ability today.

All of my students had to pick one or two shows where they would come with family or friends to be part of the audience. The first one was called, "When Was the Last Time You Called Your Mother?" One of the participants was hilarious; she was a typical over-involved mother-in-law who claimed to have no issues with her family, but then she went on to list everything she expected from them, which included coming to dinner every Friday night.

We had sessions on the blended family, starting over, going back to school as an adult; I even had the gerontologist Robert Butler appear on a show about sibling rivalry in adulthood. It was a really fun project. The segment called Starting Over had football stars Brig Owen and David Knight and women who had been stay-at-home moms. I referred to the women as CEO's of a small family business. The point was to show that whether you are a football star or a returning woman, the career issues are the same. My son was finally impressed with me when I came home after the show with signed pictures of two football stars.

That was a busy semester; I was racing from home to classes to the studio in DC, and I kept myself alive by eating candy bars out of vending machines. The six episodes were filmed over six weeks, but they were shown on consecutive days around the country. On the first show I looked pretty good. By the fifth show, I'm fat. I had to laugh at that. I always said Barbara Walters had nothing to fear from me.

After I had grown more confident as an activist, I went to visit my father in Palm Springs. This was in the early 1980s. My parents had moved there. He was chairman of the Bob Hope Golf Classic, and he invited me to come out for the tournament in January to be his hostess since my mother had recently died. It wasn't a convenient time, but I explained to my dean I had family business and needed to go.

My father took me into a trailer with all the women who were part-time staff. They would come every year to help run the event. I started talking to them and found out that they were seasonal workers with no benefits. So, I organized them; I explained to them how if they banded together and asked for what was fair and right, they could do that.

The Bob Hope Classic attracted a lot of celebrities, and my father invited me to their parties. I said, "Dad, they don't care about me and I honestly don't care about meeting them." Instead I spent a lot of time with these workers, unbeknownst to my father. After I got back home I wrote him a letter saying how proud I was of him – but I had a few points about the tournament, especially the sexism.

Those workers did speak up to the management, and they got their benefits. And every time I went back to Palm Springs, my father said, "You have to go see your constituency." He got a kick out of the whole thing.

When I got back after that first trip I was sitting in a faculty meeting, and I had a purse – a giveaway from the tournament that had "Bob Hope Golf Classic" on it. The dean looked at it and said, "Family business?"

My time at Maryland was fruitful; it was here that I developed the transitions theory that brought me notice among my academic colleagues. I still hear every week from students and scholars who say that my ideas have been important for their own work. (A summary of the theory is in Part 3.)

One of my last projects at the University of Maryland before I retired was a project on grandparents raising grandchildren, where we organized a conference to pair with the White House Conference on Aging.

It was around this time that I gave the keynote address at the gathering of college student leaders. On the next day, women being honored included the feminist Molly Yard, the Cherokee leader Wilma Mankiller, the "Shark Lady" Eugenie Clark, the gun control advocate Sarah Brady – and me, although I had already delivered my speech and had nothing more prepared. I was at the end of the alphabetical order of these luminaries and as I walked to the podium, I was trying to think of something different to say.

I told the audience, "We have heard fantastic stories of women who have persevered against great roadblocks. What you did not hear is their failures. And remember, successes have more failures than failures do."

Chapter Six

Almost Losing Myself in Denver But Testing the Transition Theory

AT ONE OF THE YEARLY CONFERENCES I organized, I asked the attendees, "How many of you have been to all the conferences?" So many raised their hands that I said, "Oh, then I can't tell my famous Denver story."

And one of them said, "The Denver story is why we keep coming back."

In 1989 I was eligible for a sabbatical at the University of Maryland. I spent the time off from teaching back at the American Council on Education, where I had been so unhappy before. By this time ACE had different leadership and I was interested in the work going on there. One day the person who headed up meetings asked me to speak at a gathering of college presidents in Denver. We set it up informally; all of the arrangements for the meeting were done in the hallway.

The week before I went to Denver I bumped into her, again in the hallway. I mentioned that I would be there on Friday and go right from the airport to the speech. I remember that in the cab I put contacts in my eyes so I'd be ready; all I would have to do was put on lipstick and give my talk.

When I arrived at the hotel, I couldn't find the meeting. At the front desk, they knew nothing about it. I was shocked. So I called my office and they said, "Oh my, Nancy; the meeting is in November. This is October!"

I couldn't believe I had made such a huge mistake. I called Steve and got him out of a meeting and burst into tears – what every feminist does, right? Steve said, "Nancy, you cannot fall apart in Denver. Your book, *Overwhelmed*, just came out and it would be terrible for sales. Why don't you follow your own advice when it comes to dealing with a setback?"

After talking to Steve, I wandered across the street to the Brown Palace, a more elegant hotel. I sat down and the maitre d' asked what he could do. I blurted out that I was in town a month early, and couldn't get a reservation to fly back home right away. He brought me a cocktail.

"I don't drink," I said. "Certainly not in the middle of the day."

"You do today," he said.

I sat there with my drink and asked myself, "Is there anything at all in my book that would help me cope? Or is my book just meaningless?"

Then I remembered the exact two pages I needed, where I had written that when you are faced with a challenging situation, you have to ask yourself three questions:

Can I change the situation? Obviously, I couldn't change this one, I thought: October is October. And even if I hired the best lawyer in the world she could not turn October into November!

Can I change the way I look at it? Well, I could do that. After all, on that day I wasn't just a dowdy professor; I was sipping a cocktail in a beautiful old hotel in downtown Denver. If I wanted to, I could fly to San Francisco for lunch, and then to Paris for breakfast. And I even had a great opening line for my speech when I came back next month: "You have never had a speaker more eager to speak to you."

How can I deal with the stress of my situation? By this time, the answer came easily. I took a nice, aerobic walk up and down the walking street, and went in and out of stores, buying things. And this is how I got myself out of Denver. From that time on, I had my formula for handling an unpleasant surprise: If something happens muse, can I change it? Can I change the way I see it? And how can I make myself relax?

Overwhelmed was my first venture writing for the popular press. I was a tenured full professor, so the pressure to write strictly academic books was lessened.

My life was overwhelming – two young children, a husband with a national-international career, full-time work. I was doing multiple studies of different kinds of transitions and simultaneously writing a textbook, *Counseling Adults in Transition*. I wanted to translate what I knew into helpful, useful formats. However, I had no idea how to find a popular publisher so I just kept sending out proposals.

I learned to take rejection by countering with persistence. I will never forget the thrill when I got a call from a woman saying, "We want your book."

The message of *Overwhelmed* is that everyone experiences transitions, whether they are events or non-events, anticipated or unanticipated. These transitions, like the birth of a child or retiring, alter our lives – our roles, relationships, routines and assumptions. Transitions take time, and people's reactions to them change, for better or worse, while they are underway.

At first, people think of nothing but being a new graduate, a new parent, a new widow, a recent retiree. Then they begin to separate from the past and move toward the new role, for a while teetering between the two – what anthropologists call a period of liminality. The process of leaving one set of roles, relationships, routines, and assumptions and establishing new ones takes time. Many people flounder, looking for the right niche, even after years. How, then, do we handle this journey, live through it and learn from it?

My unsettling experience in Denver was resolved by means of what I called in my book the "4 S System." These are your potential resources for coping. The first "S" refers to a person's Situation at the time of transition. For example, if you decide to relocate to another city and your significant other becomes ill in the midst of the move, this adds an element of stress to a transition that you had wanted and planned. In Denver, the fact that I was in the right place at the wrong time transformed a situation I had looked forward to into one that made me doubt my own competence.

The second "S" is Self: a person's inner strength for coping with a situation. Optimism, resilience and the ability to deal with ambiguity are factors that help in dealing with the unexpected, and people who develop these resources will fare better.

The third "S" refers to the Support available at the time of transition, and this is critical to one's sense of well-being. If a new retiree, for example, moves to a new city knowing no one, with no support network, the adaptation could take longer.

And the fourth "S" has to do with one's Strategic response to the transition. There is no magic coping strategy, and the person who uses lots of strategies flexibly will be better able to cope.

When contemplating a major transition – going back to school as an adult, say, or changing careers or retiring – one can look at one's 4 S's and ask: Is my Situation good at this time? Do I bring a resilient Self to the move? Is a Support system available to me? Do I have lots of coping Strategies in my repertoire? If all S's are positive, a move might be a good decision. However, with a problematic situation or minimal supports, there might be a decision to delay the move until one builds supports in the new community and one's situation improves.

With the help of Stephanie Kay, former student, then colleague, now friend, we developed a self-scoring inventory to assess your resources for coping, The Transition Guide. This allows you to see which resources are working for you and which ones need strengthening.

What is now known as the Schlossberg Transition Theory took many years to develop, and my own life served as a constant inspiration. Back in graduate school at Columbia, I had discovered the theories of Robert K. Merton, which dealt with how individuals become socialized into their adult roles. He focused on students becoming doctors. The subject of adult socialization intrigued me. My intellectual deadness as an undergrad at Barnard was upended and I got excited about ideas again.

But it was much later that I began focusing on transitions – as a result of my own confusion. I found myself in the midst of a positive, voluntary transition: moving back to DC from Detroit. I had taken a very prestigious job in DC as the first woman executive of the American Council on Education. I should have been happy. So why was I upset? This mystery started me on the four-decade evolution of my theory.

The move back to DC happened after Walter Reuther was killed in a plane crash. Steve and Leonard Woodcock, who had succeeded Walter, decided the UAW needed a presence in Washington. I landed this marvelous job at the American Council on Education, as its first female executive; it could not have been more gratifying. I was reunited with my best friend Janet, and we had a fantastic house that faced a forest.

And yet I was miserable.

That led me to sit down with my friend Sue Smock, a sociologist and researcher in Detroit, and said, "I don't understand why I'm not on Cloud 9."

Sue was very significant in my life. I had met her in a bookstore when I first moved to Detroit: I was looking for *Daedalus* magazine. This woman was standing next to me and we started talking. We had a fun conversation, and I thought, "Oh, she's someone I would like to know." Later, we reconnected at a lecture and she became my closest friend in town. We were neurotic mothers together, and spent hours on the phone processing. We were so nutty.

When I told Sue about my quandary regarding the move to DC, she said, "We're going to make a laundry list of all the things that happen in a transition." Our conversation that day helped me formulate the transition theory – part of it, anyway.

Because of my own experience, my first transition study was about geographical moving. I didn't want the death of a child, or something extraordinary; I wanted to look at what happens to a person during a normal, expected and even desirable transition. I never published that study; I was just testing out some of the ideas that would lead to my transition theory and the 4 S System.

To find out how people develop the resilience that helps them weather a geographical move, I compared the experiences of military families, who expected multiple moves, and civilian ones. I remember interviewing one military wife: It was 1974, and the women's movement was flourishing. She said her husband had been posted to a new location and they were supposed to move – but this time she wasn't going. She said she had moved 18 times, and she was finished with that. I was listening to her but in my head, I assumed her refusal was because of the women's movement.

I said, "Tell me why this time is different." She said, "I can't move; I'm having an affair."

I was beginning to figure out that life will surprise you, that every transition is unique to the individual, that you should always question your assumptions. And that's how the whole thing started.

Overwhelmed launched me into the more popular arena and I began to see myself as a translator – developing an academic theory and translating it for the person on the street. When the book came out, I was asked to be on Oprah's talk show, but I explained that one of my doctoral students had her oral exams scheduled for the day they wanted me to come. So much for making the big time!

In 1996, my second general-interest book – *Going to Plan B* – was published by Simon & Schuster. This book grew out of my growing interest in a particular kind of transition, a concept that was understudied: non-events. These are the transitions you had every reason to expect but did not occur.

With graduate students and a small grant from the university, I studied all kinds of non-events. Some are the result of someone else (like not becoming a grandparent, not becoming King of England); some are your own (not getting pregnant, not getting promoted), and some are the result of a major event (a car accident that leads to becoming disabled and not having the career or personal life you planned, or not having your expected wedding because of the pandemic).

Many non-events are delayed. I thought I was having a non-event because I had no grandchildren. Now I have three of them – what I called a non-event became a delayed event.

Believe it or not, there was a bidding war for that book and Simon & Schuster won. This time, I told my students that if Oprah asked me back on her show for *Plan B*, I would have to say yes. My event was getting a great publisher; my non-event was that the publisher asked me to go on a book tour and then canceled – and Oprah never invited me a second time. But I lived through that by remembering that successes have more failures than failures do!

Dr. Sue Smock

Stephanie Kay, Nancy Schlossberg
The 4 S System

Chapter Seven

Discovering How Not to Retire

AFTER STEVE RETIRED FROM THE UAW, he joined a consulting firm. He was still making speeches but was feeling less relevant.

We had owned a place on Longboat Key in Sarasota, very unfancy. We would rent it out most of the time. Steve had found like-minded people here, mostly from the labor movement, and there was a sense of camaraderie. He was really the one who pushed us to move here, but I was not unhappy about it. In fact, I had already given retirement a lot of thought.

When I was in my late 60s, fully functioning as a professor, I had an eye-opening experience. After a retirement party of a vibrant woman in her mid-70s, I was walking back to my office with two deans. They discussed that she should have retired so much earlier. I thought, "No one is going to say that about me." That started me on the path of thinking about my next adventure.

Rituals are important in a major transition like retirement. I remember when I was leaving the university, my secretary put all my awards in a box for me to take home. I told her, "Throw them away; that was then." Thinking about the past doesn't help you. It's more about the future and what you can do.

For me it's important to have a future with a purpose, and to make a difference.

Luckily for me, money was not an issue. The issue was my life, my identity. I had always worked, even when the children were young. Work and family were my life. I loved my work. Who would I be when I stopped? How would I organize my life?

I figured that it would be easy for me since I had studied transitions. Right? Wrong. Everyone knows you don't plan two major transitions simultaneously, but I left my job and moved to Sarasota with Steve at the same time. Suddenly my entire world was changed. I moved into a new role or, I should say, no role.

I left those I had worked with and many friends and family, and was faced with entirely new routines and confusion about who I was and my purpose in life. I was used to the status of being a professor, of not having to explain myself. When I moved to my new community I felt impatient to find a new life. I had forgotten what I knew – that the process of leaving or exiting a role that had been major and finding a new role, relationships, routines and assumptions is a process over time. It takes time. I wanted it *now*. I felt lonely and at sea.

I had assumed many nonprofits in Sarasota would want to hire me. Wrong again. They wanted my money and my volunteer services, not my expertise. Eventually, as I started meeting people, I was recruited for board memberships, not for a work role. I wanted to work.

In addition to feeling purposeless, I was not used to being with Steve during the day. I missed my children, my colleagues. I was unhappy.

It took me a few years to find my place, to develop a network of friends, to find a purpose. But the process of exiting my life as a professor and living through a period of confusion until re-establishing a new set of roles, relationships, routines and assumptions produced a great deal of soul-searching.

I was surprised that I had not realized that retirement is a major set of transitions. I should have been prepared. One way I coped was by interviewing retirees and running some focus groups. This resulted in two books on retirement, a new purpose and better understanding of this complex transition.

In Cortez, an old fishing village near Sarasota, there was a trailer park where someone I knew introduced me to the residents. Most of my interviewees were blue-collar workers. I remember one man saying, "My wife and I never had time to see each other. We worked different shifts, and we would leave post-its for each other." In retirement, their life was wonderful.

I also did some interviews at the World Bank in Washington, and the issue was the whole identity change that retirement brings. They were not particularly happy campers.

During these interviews I came up with the paths that people take after leaving full-time work: Continuers, Adventurers, Involved Spectators, Searchers, Easy Gliders, and Retreaters The basic issues, no matter which path you are on, include developing a new identity, forming new relationships and identifying your purpose. Money and health are clearly critical.

I discovered that understanding retirement was not necessarily related to age. Tell me you're 60, and that tells me nothing. What transitions are you dealing with? That's the way to get a handle on what is going on with you.

One major transition that often accompanies retirement is more involvement with grandchildren. When my first granddaughter, Robin, arrived, Larry, Robin's father, and his son got pneumonia and had to move out, so I went to help Karen.

It was kind of scary: I was not competent to feed the goats on Karen's farm. Larry, half-dead from pneumonia, would come at night and take care of them.

Karen needed baby gear, including a diaper pail, and the only store nearby was Walmart. There were two taboos Steve felt strongly about as a consumer; one was buying foreign cars not made by union workers, and the other was that he would never go to Walmart because of the way it treated employees. It would have been easier telling him I was having an affair than that I was going to Walmart. At the checkout I started giving the poor girl a lecture about workers' rights. She finally said, "I can't discuss this with you."

When I got back from shopping it was nighttime. I opened the trunk and carried the baby items piece by piece into the farmhouse. When I finished I slammed the trunk, and Karen's cat had jumped into it and screamed. It was a Sunday night, and I had to get the cat to an emergency vet. I called Mark and he rushed out and found a vet to take care of her. The cat lived. It was frantic.

I was so involved in Robin's early days, and I felt such love for this little thing. It was chaotic, with Karen trying to nurse and the goats screaming. Karen and I had a fight because I wanted to hire somebody to come help her. She won; I lost.

Michele, Nancy and Stevie

I ended up with three marvelous grandchildren. Robin is spiritual and a nurturer; Jenny an adventurer and a thinker; Stevie a talented performer. They are very meaningful in my life. My presence matters to them, and it's a reason to keep wanting to live. I like to talk to them, explore their worlds and be part of their lives. As I got older they became more important to me.

In addition to the shift in one's focus on family, known as "kinkeeping," many retirees turn

Jenny

Robin

to travel as a way of bringing meaning and passion to this phase of their lives. Travel offers opportunities not only for adventure, but also for learning and growth. One vivid memory is the last trip I took with Steve, ten years before he died. Remarkably, it took place in September 2001, so I was en route from Tanzania when 9/11 happened. Other adventures included traveling to Japan when they translated *Overwhelmed* into Japanese, to Australia, France, England, the West coast, Mexico and even some spas. We were invited to visit China when Leonard Woodcock was its first ambassador but unfortunately my back was so bad I could not travel.

The Safari to Tanzania was memorable on so many levels. It started when we were at Janet and Paul Duke's for dinner in Sarasota with an interesting group. One thing led to another, and we decided to go on a safari. I went on the Safari with friends where we ended up surrounded by elephants, monkeys, lions, gazelles and many animals I had never seen before.

Our safari guide was Lynne Leakey, the former daughter-in-law of the noted anthropologists Louis and Mary Leakey. We had a group of 12 – all fascinating friends – and a very attractive and knowledgeable guide, so life was perfect. When an elephant mother protecting her baby approached our jeep flapping her ears, we held our breaths and prayed. But the most

Janet and Paul Duke

memorable adventure of the trip was even more unexpected.

Leading the safari was a pleasant Tanzanian, who told me about his young son. The youth wanted to study at the one school in his country that offered training in wildlife protection. But the application for a scholarship at this school was daunting.

A balloon ride had been arranged, with a departure before dawn. Our Tanzanian guide was free, so I said to Paul Duke, "Why don't you and I forgo the balloon ride, so we can sit down with this man and his son to help with the application form?" We did, and found the process so bureaucratic that we

decided to raise the $4,000 for tuition ourselves.

With the help of our entrepreneurial friend Bob Bernhard, who could solve all sorts of problems, we contacted an agency to whom we could give the money, to be passed on to the school. All was set; we headed home feeling that we had made a difference.

I flew from Tanzania to Rome where I was met by Steve, along with Jeanne Nunn and her companion Bernie Freid.

We laughed all the way to Pagonico, where our friends had rented a villa. When we arrived they greeted us, all looking defeated and some of them crying. It was 9/11 but we did not know it. When they told us what had happened, we were stunned. I will never forget our reactions. We felt so frightened – not for our personal safety but for our way of life.

We went to town to find a TV and saw bodies jumping out of buildings. After a few days, we went to Florence where we could watch TV in English.

In October, back in the States, I received a frantic phone call from Lynne Leakey. The Tanzanian boy was turned away from the school because the money never arrived. It was like a bad dream. I called the pass-through agency and the contact person was on leave. Calls to the school went unanswered. I was determined to solve the problem; it became my part-time job.

Finally, the money was located and the young boy went to school. For many years following his graduation, I received this message: "Dear Madam, I just saved some animals from poachers. Thank you so much."

Throughout my own retirement, the critical issue has been the need to matter. Morris Rosenberg, the late distinguished sociologist from the University of Maryland, coined the phrase "mattering" – the need to feel noticed, appreciated, and depended upon – as one that describes a universal, and often overlooked, motive that influences our thinking and behavior.

When I was still at Maryland, I had a student gave me an article by Morris. It was a meta-analysis of boys, some of whom became delinquent and some who didn't. Morris came up with a notion that it's not about self-concept, because that goes up and down. Instead, he thought, the boys' fates had to do with mattering.

At the end of his article he wrote a throwaway paragraph about retirees and mattering. I made an appointment and met with him and said how fascinated I was with his work. He said, "Join me; my students are focusing on homelessness." I said my students would want to talk about higher education and mattering. I worked with a professor in the measurement department for help to develop a mattering scale. We found that if an adult student doesn't feel he or she matters, it's more likely that person will drop out.

Morris was writing a book; I saw the manuscript before he died. I know it existed, but unfortunately the copy was never found. When I used his concept as a way of understanding who flourishes in retirement, it resonated with a lot of people. Rosenberg's work gave me the bottom line about retirement— the need to matter, to feel relevant, still noticed and depended upon.

It is critical to believe that we count in others' lives and feel we make a difference to them. Morris Rosenberg suggested, and I found, that retirees who no longer feel appreciated do not do as well as those who feel connected and recognize their significance. They want to feel important and part of something important. The concept explains why some retirees are happy and others experience retirement as "perplexing" – as a punishment instead of the reward they were expecting.

The book that launched my encore career was *Retire Smart Retire Happy* (2004). It became the centerpiece for a PBS pledge special with the Boston station. It was so exciting and the show ran for 13 months.

My publisher, APA, asked me to update the work. Instead of a second edition, I was asked to write a new book, *Revitalizing Retirement* (2009). The second book looked at issues of happiness and mattering. I had done many studies about the importance of people to feel they matter to others, that they are noticed and cared for. This is especially true for retirees.

I felt I mattered to the University; I felt irrelevant when I first retired. It took a while to develop a life filled with activities and projects. Over time, I finally felt that I mattered again.

Retirement party given by Stephanie Kay and
Mary Ann Beatty with Sylvia Rosenfield,
Susanne Sedge, Elly Waters, Jan Birk and others.

Mary Ann, Nancy and Stephanie

Retirement Party Cake

Chapter Eight

My Life as a Widow in Waiting

WHEN I WAS IN MY LATE 70S AND EARLY 80S, I went through a crisis I call being a widow in waiting. It all started when I was summoned to a DC hospital emergency room, where my husband was taken after falling down a 188-foot-high escalator at the Dupont Circle Metro station.

The doctors stitched Steve up, but he was never the same after the accident. First he used a cane, then a walker, and finally a wheelchair. Then came a pacemaker, hip and knee replacements, a heart bypass, minor surgeries and dementia. So for more than six years before he died in 2011, I became a caregiver as much as a wife, while he experienced what seemed like a never-ending series of medical crises. I became a widow-in-waiting.

For many widows in waiting, life is suspended. Several years before Steve's fall, we had put our apartment on the market and placed a deposit on an apartment in a retirement community, thinking it would be good for Steve to be in a protected environment with activities on the premises. Two weeks after the realtor began marketing our apartment, we found that Steve was internally bleeding. I panicked, canceled the apartment in the retirement community and took our apartment off the market – much to the realtor's dismay.

I canceled a business trip to South Dakota because, at the time, Steve appeared to be actively dying. Then I canceled my trip to Las Vegas to help my close friend celebrate her big birthday because Steve was having emergency palliative hernia surgery. Then my close, close friend Mickey Bazelon Knox died. I wanted to go to her funeral but stayed home instead.

Steve's quality of life continued to diminish. He always knew me and the children, and was well aware of his surroundings. I decided I would keep him at home no matter what. He needed round-the-clock care because he was too heavy for me to move, and he could no longer take care of his daily needs.

I constantly experienced opposing emotions. I wanted Steve to live; I wanted him to die; I wanted to be with him all the time, I wanted to be out doing things; I wanted time to stand still. I wanted time to fast-forward so I could figure out what I want to do with whatever time I had. I needed knee surgery since I was in pain, but I didn't want to be immobilized.

Many caregivers report conflicts between at least one other member of the family who sees the situation differently than the main caregiver. Steve wanted more surgeries in order to get better. Our son Mark argued that his father's voice should be heard. I loved that Mark was fighting for his father, even though I was now in the position of opposing both Steve and Mark. It is difficult to stand up to other members of the family – difficult because you feel so vulnerable and unsure about what to do.

Why not let Steve decide for himself, asked Mark? Unfortunately, the social workers in Hospice determined that Steve had dementia, and was unable to make wise medical decisions.

At one point, my husband had such pain, but otherwise was not deteriorating. I got permission from Hospice to take him to his urologist and his hernia specialist, hoping they could tell me how to make him more comfortable without surgery – but the hernia specialist advised a second palliative surgery. I felt so alone. I knew if I opted for surgery, he would have to leave Hospice.

I had been so definite about no more surgery, even fighting about it. To my amazement, his long-term doctor felt that a palliative surgery to relieve him of pain would be a good idea, since he had not died as expected. I went along with it; he had the surgery and was home in a day, in great pain.

I was scared. Would Hospice take us back? I remembered worrying about my children getting admitted into the right colleges, but I never thought I would be trying to pull strings to get us back into Hospice. Luckily, my husband's doctor gave an order for readmission.

At first my coping was dysfunctional. I had two car accidents. The second was when I was rushing home; I drove into the bus station and ripped a city sign right out of its concrete. I had to go to traffic school, pay an enormous fee, and see my insurance premium raised. The good news was that I did not hurt anyone – just my car. This served as a wake-up call: I was not coping well.

Transitions waiting to happen include uncertainty, ambiguity and loss of control. Although my future was uncertain and ambiguous, I spent time thinking about my life without my husband. Would I stay in our apartment? Would I downsize? Would I move back to DC? I was helped by remembering the work of Bernice Neugarten who found that women in late middle age prepare themselves for this transition by rehearsing for widowhood. I was doing just that.

It helped me to talk to others in the same boat. And books helped: I felt as if I were reading my story when I read Gail Sheehy's *Passages in Caregiving: Turning Chaos into Confidence*. Her identification of the "in-between stage," including the complicated emotions and decisions she had to make, resonated with me.

I looked at my husband one night, struggling to breathe. He told me he wanted to stay alive to help me. I counted my blessings – to have had a special husband who worked to make a difference in the world, who fought for workers' rights and civil rights, and who always showed his love for me.

But the caregiving had an effect on me. In 2009, two years before Steve died, I wrote in my journal: "I am turning 80 in a few months. Eighty – a number reserved for the very old, wrinkled, bent-over people we see hobbling along ... This is the first birthday that has had an emotional impact on me. I have been happy with every other birthday. I was still productive, writing books, speaking to groups, involved. Now life is different; my last book has been written and will be published this spring. This is the first time since 1984 that I have not had a book project, that I have not had an idea I was eager to pursue. That is probably why this birthday is so daunting."

But thanks to my participation in a water aerobics group called "The Mermaids," I received valuable support in reframing that birthday. I casually mentioned to them that I would love to walk across Sarasota's John Ringling Bridge with my son and daughter-in-law, but with a torn meniscus and not much stamina, I feared I would never make it all the way across and back.

Then our aerobics teacher, Kathleen, got on the case. She suggested meeting me on one side of the bridge while Jane, a fellow Mermaid, parked on the opposite end. The morning of the big day, with water bottle in hand, I met Kathleen and two others in the group, Linda and Richard. We started up the bridge; I felt tentative but safe. When we saw Jane walking from her side to help me turn back if I needed to, a decision had to be made. I heard myself saying, "Let's go for the whole bridge."

We made it, and more group members were waiting with a big placard: "Happy Birthday Nancy." At a gazebo under the bridge, there were birthday napkins and plates, champagne, orange juice and coffee cake. This experience helped me welcome my 80th birthday.

My family came to Sarasota, and each day we had a special event. I walked the bridge with Mark and my daughter-in-law Michele, and the next night we had a dinner celebration. Sue Smock surprised us with a bottle of champagne, and Steve asked everyone to say something about me. The one I remember most was my granddaughter Robin, who said she loved her grammy because I loved her.

Now I know that I would not trade the last two years of Steve's life for anything. We would listen to music, hold hands, and just be together. He was always in good humor and appreciative for all we did for him.

When the inevitable happened and Steve died, I was actually in a rehab center following emergency back surgery and waiting for a hip replacement. Mark came and got me out of the center at night so I could be with Steve before he died. I will never forget that night. I was in hospital clothing and Steve could barely talk. He said, "You have to tell Mark to take me to Detroit to help the new president of the UAW save the labor movement."

With that he closed his eyes, and Mark took me back to the rehab center. My son and daughter-in-law had stayed with him every minute during the dying process and our daughter had visited often, comforting us both. Strangely, my being ill was a blessing. I was in a cocoon for four months.

Being "out of time" removed me from the normal routines of life, and provided a protected period to grieve. I moved back into time gradually – first with care at home, then lots of physical therapy and learning to walk again. I gave two memorials for Steve—one when I was in a wheel chair in the lobby of the Sarabande and five months later, with my recovery well underway, I arranged a memorial for him in DC – a celebration of Steve, his life, and his contributions to the labor movement. I felt that this ritual was important in enabling me and others in the family to move ahead into a new phase of life.

My husband was ill during the writing of my book, *Revitalizing Retirement*; he died in 2011. I always expected to return to DC after Steve died, but I stayed in Sarasota because I had become so involved in the life of the city – as a board member of the Asolo Theatre and the Women's Resource Center, SCOPE and one of the founders of the Institute for the Ages. I just could not leave Sarasota.

By then I was no longer a widow in waiting, a distraught widow, or someone with medical problems. I was becoming the same optimistic person I had always been, but I was now carving out a new life, strengthened by almost 50 years in a marriage filled with love, romance, fun and excitement. I was ready to move on, and I did.

I had been raised to be independent, so I didn't have the problem some new widows have in being overwhelmed with loneliness. I did really well for 10 or 12 years during Steve's illness and afterward – keeping busy, traveling, working hard to establish female relationships in Sarasota. Then a radical change occurred: I became intensely conscious of being "one."

Many things stopped being fun to do on my own – traveling to new places with no one to share the discovery, attending functions as a single, taking a trip that required substantial preparation and having no one to share that burden. Feeling lonely prompted me to develop strategies that would change my situation.

Chapter Nine

Embracing the Present, and the Future

IN 1996, MY BOOK *Going to Plan B* (Simon & Schuster) had just been published and my daughter was about to turn 30. When she learned that my book discussed non-event transitions – those transitions you had every right to expect that do not occur – she cried out, "I am a walking non-event! I do not have a husband or children or a farm and I am about to turn 30." She was so distraught.

Even if she could do nothing immediately about the children or the husband, I asked, "Can you have a piece of the dream?" After thinking about it, she realized that she could sell her condo and buy a small farm. That was 25 years ago. Now she has a working goat farm, a wonderful husband and two marvelous children. She realized she had some control over at least part of her life. It relieved her, dissipated her depression and gave her the impetus to move on.

Karen's goat farm, Avalon Springs Farm

The take away: When life is not following your plan, when dreams for your life seem doomed, when depression becomes a prominent part of your life, realize that you can look at your dreams and figure out a small part that you can work on now.

This is why, several years after losing Steve, I decided to address my loneliness, and succumbed to the suggestions of friends by signing up for online dating. As I got into a nightly routine of checking Match.com and JDate.com, one man's profile kept popping up. When he contacted me, we started getting to know each other through daily emails.

Nancy and Ron

Ron's sense of humor became evident when he suggested we meet and he offered to pick me up. He persisted, and finally I said, "Will you tell me if you are a murderer or a rapist?" He responded that he definitely was not a murderer – and I agreed to have him pick me up. Just to be safe, before we went out, I gave all the information I had about him to Gail Levin, a close friend telling her if she did not hear from me by 4 p.m. pull out all the stops!

We started dating and introduced each other to our adult children and our friends. We found shared interests in the love of music, travel, dancing and theater. When he turned 90, I was at the party to celebrate with his entire family at a Club Med.

After a year of dating, Ron moved into my apartment. When we decided to live together we agreed that neither of us would be caregivers again. After all, we had both already outlived the life expectancy that statisticians assigned us. If care were required, we would move close to one of our children. As we aged, we moved to a retirement community with some services. Ron and my son Mark did not understand why I wanted to move. I was active and as they said, "not ready." But based on what I knew about aging, I knew it was better to be in a community and be there *before* you needed it. So we moved to Sarasota Bay Club, the best thing I ever did.

Too Young to be Old, my latest and last book, came at a time when a major project in which I was centrally involved failed. I was one of the founders of the Institute for the Ages and at the time of its belly-up was chair of the board.

I got involved in starting the institute through Tim Dutton, who was the CEO of a local public-private nonprofit called SCOPE – Sarasota County Openly Plans for Excellence. Tim was the best I ever worked with – imaginative, creative, and supportive. We used to run these conferences about aging, the Winter Forums. That was really a continuation of what I did at Wayne State and Maryland.

We brought in lots of expert speakers, and probably the most meaningful to the community was the late geriatric psychiatrist Gene Cohen who talked about creativity and aging. Tim organized a group of us to talk about how these forums might evolve: Pam Baron, her husband Art Mahoney, Roxanne Joffe and several others. We started meeting at the Northern Trust bank building every Friday morning, and came up with the idea for the institute.

The institute failed because of many factors including finances; it was the wrong business model. To get county money we said we would become self-supporting and provide a certain number of jobs. A major benefactor backed out, and I happened to be chair of the board when it all fell apart. I had wanted the position; I only got it when things were going south.

I don't know whether it was true or my imagination, but suddenly I felt like I was a pariah and nobody wanted to have anything to do with me. I had been very invested in the project and blamed myself, along with the rest of the board, for its demise.

I have a lot of skills, but what I don't have are administrative and political talents. I can deal with anxiety, but not hostility. I'm much better at creating things and ideas, and I made a mistake taking on that leading role. I felt terrible.

Then I remembered another time I had stepped outside of my skill set, when I was a graduate student at Columbia. They needed someone to come to Auburn University for the summer to teach a course in tests and measurements. I needed the money, so I took the job, but I had actually gotten a D in statistics in college. The lesson I learned: Don't do something you don't know how to do at all.

I think if you don't have too many failures, the ones you have offer a learning experience. That's important for young people to know.

After a period of retreating from public life in Sarasota. I needed a new project, something to help me with the move to the Bay Club and the demise of the institute. I decided to write a final book, *Too Young to be Old*, putting down my thoughts about aging and transitions.

In addition to an overview of transition theory, age bias, and all the personal and public transitions older people experience, I made this book personal. I included two short memoirs – one about Steve's illness and death and one about my new romance with Ron. Writing the book gave me a great deal of satisfaction and brought me back to speaking and volunteering.

For a while after our move, Ron and I really enjoyed the sociability and activities of the retirement community. But then signs that something was amiss with Ron began to appear. He would get lost when driving to familiar places; he could no longer handle his finances; he began sleeping for hours in the daytime, and he stopped talking in social situations.

I did not know how to make the necessary changes occur. It was almost harder to hurt someone else than to be hurt. I knew it would upset and confuse him, so I had just let things drag on.

Eventually I had to acknowledge the seriousness of his condition. At the same time, my daughter needed an involved medical procedure and I had to travel back and forth between Florida and Maryland. Ron's daughter and I agreed that he would move to live with her in Virginia near his grandchildren. She eventually found a nearby facility that allowed dogs so that he and his longtime dog companion Stella could be together.

But when I saw photos of the pictures in Ron's new apartment and I was not in any of them, I felt I had been erased. After talking to Ron's daughter Fern we agreed it was too upsetting for Ron to see pictures of me or even see me in person. I was shocked and then overtaken by a feeling of emptiness when I realized I no longer existed in Ron's world.

How could this have happened when we'd been together for five years?

It was very hard and lonely without Ron and his dog Stella. But time is a great healer. Karen finally had her surgery – after delays because of insurance. It was a great success even though the recovery

Luna

Stella

was difficult and long. I got used to living alone.

I realized several things: I needed to have something living in my apartment. I have always been a dog person, but at 91, I took the leap and got a beautiful ragdoll cat – supposedly the breed most like a dog. We named him Luna, after the llama that had been on Karen's farm since the very beginning and had protected the goats when they were giving birth.

It took me several months to learn how to communicate with Luna; cats operate on their own terms. But over the last three years Luna and I have worked out a lovely relationship. We have daily and nightly rituals, and play times, and I love her.

During this time, Richard and Sheila Olin became my neighbors. Sheila had full-blown dementia and they moved here to find a safer place for her. They were an adorable couple – always walking with arms entwined. They both loved to visit and play with Luna.

One day – I don't know why I did this – I asked them if they knew anyone for me to meet. In a few days, Richard came back with a suggestion; but I vaguely knew the man and was not interested. Sadly, Sheila died right before Christmas. I invited Richard to join us for the holiday meal, telling him he could just show up at the last minute. He did. Later, my son referred to Richard as "the aging Hippie."

In time, Richard started to call and ask me, "Are you

receiving?" I often was busy for dinner, but he would come in for drinks and a chat. We became good friends, talking about everything from career aspirations to loneliness, and what we wanted out of life.

One night, after about eight months, I asked Richard what he thought was going on in our relationship. "Love," he said. I did not respond; I was taken aback. But the next time I saw him I said, "I think you used a four-letter word to describe our relationship." And that was the beginning.

Richard is a wonderful man and artist. I encouraged him to enter his work in art shows and he started calling me his muse. One of his sculptures is called LAT: living apart together. And that is what we do. We each need our own space, but are in a committed partnership. I feel so fortunate to have someone in my life with whom I can be open, and I have come to rely on him in many ways. These words describe him: creative, caring, competent, open.

One night I had a crazy dream: I was having a party but needed to get all my furniture out of the storage unit in my building. However, another group was having a function so it was hard to find my things. Finally, a valet said my storage unit had nothing in it. I was a little upset with myself for not dealing with this before the party, and scared that I had not documented all the furniture that was in storage. I thought about canceling, but then I knew what I would do: just get card tables and chairs and let the party proceed. I think this dream reflects my modus operandi. I can feel I have lost everything, but then I modify and go to Plan B.

I find that as I get older, the possibilities of having plans go awry, or of big bumps in the road, seem much less important. I don't feel the need to control everything as I did before. There's almost always a Plan B, waiting to surprise me.

Chapter Ten

Not Quite the Final Surprise

Marianne, Michele, Stevie, Nancy, Mark

THERE IS AN ENORMOUS DIFFERENCE between your 80s and your 90s. You want things to be stable and last forever, but there is no forever. Living in a retirement community is both comforting and upsetting; you are so aware of people dying all the time. You develop a new friendship, start sharing your vulnerabilities, start caring – and then it is over.

It does not make sense that older individuals are happier than younger people. After all, I am 94 and have experienced many losses – my husband; Norma Sue, my best friend from junior high school; and other close friends like Jeanne Nunn and Mickey Knox. My life with those I knew most intimately no longer exists.

And in your later years you often come tantalizingly close to death yourself. Last summer I suddenly felt unwell and found myself in an intensive care unit, diagnosed with Covid 19 and pneumonia. The doctors told Mark I would likely not survive the week. I do remember being "out of time," very far away – and deciding that my friends and family were worth the effort of returning to full consciousness. Many parts of my body were affected, and the slow recovery tested my patience.

So how could I be happier now than when I was young? It makes no sense.

And yet today as I was sitting in the garden at the retirement community where I live, looking at the beautiful garden facing the bay filled with sailboats, I was as calm and happy as I had ever been.

I have experienced many transitions, faced many challenges, spent many nights crying because those to whom I was most attached have died. Why am I happy? Why is Marcia, my best friend at age 12, and one of the few close friends still alive, able to handle her life at age 95 after the loss of her grandson with whom she was very close and her lover of eight years, plus most of her friends? She said, "I can't explain it but I am not depressed. Is something wrong with me?"

Laura Carstensen, professor of psychology and founding director of the Stanford Center on Longevity, explains this paradox. We have perspective. We have dealt with many challenges so have developed some skill in handling life. I have experienced divorce, widowhood, death of close friends, unrequited love, lots of successes and failures along the way. Now that I am 94, I selected an excellent place to live, my children are in a good place, my grandchildren are developing beautifully; and probably most important to my daily satisfaction, I have a special friend Richard.

Friendship means a great deal to me. Mickey Bazelon Knox and Bob Knox created the cover showing pictures of all the books I've written. Sue Tolchin gave me an 80th birthday party in DC and the invitations specified no gifts. Mickey didn't care. Bob called my department at the University of Maryland and got the chair and asked for a grad assistant to get pictures of the covers. That gave me something to leave my family. That's my legacy, these books.

My long life has taught me some things that I want to share with my three granddaughters Robin, Jenny and Stevie. If others are interested, if my stories touch them as they struggle with the issues we all face, then the effort will have been worth it. I guess the important thing I want them to know is that their paths are not set. As I write this, Robin just graduated from high school, about to take a gap year as she figures out what to do. Jenny is thinking of ways to have adventures and make a difference. Stevie is excelling in competitive dancing. Their lives keep evolving. Each one is so special and I hope to be around a bit longer so I can see the creative ways they will carve out their lives.

Most important is my current relationship with my adult children and their families Karen, Larry, Robin and Jenny; and Mark, Michele and Stevie. A special shout-out to Larry my son-in-law and Michele my beautiful daughter-in-law.

Just recently, I had a meltdown, which never happens. Because of health complications, likely resulting from my bout with Covid, I had to cancel a trip to DC I had been looking forward to. Then I had trouble catching my cat so I could take him to the vet, and then my housekeeper called to let me know I had paid her twice. I thought: I'm on my way down. So, I

Robin, Jenny, Larry, and Karen

went and got an iced tea at Starbucks and sat by the water to meditate. Then I started to question whether I really wanted to live. Suddenly, however, I realized that I had to rush home to go to the bathroom, because of all that tea. The whole thing became absolutely hilarious and those thoughts disappeared.

It is rare for me to have a meltdown, but sometimes things escalate. I knew this was something I should talk over with my children, and get the support I needed. My son Mark helped me focus on the aspects of my health that I can still control. For instance, I had a doctor's appointment for the end of the month. I decided to move the appointment to an earlier date, and have Mark come with me. Karen was empathetic and basically gave me support and love.

This episode reminded me of how wonderful it is to have adult children whom you really trust, to whom you can show your vulnerabilities. They don't come rushing in to say, "You need help." They make a few points – empathetic, caring, loving – but they don't try to take over my life.

Mark and Nancy

About three years ago I had a car accident, and I said to Mark, "Maybe I should give up driving." It was a hot summer day; as I was driving slowly across a quiet intersection, something banged my car. I saw a man lying on the ground; I didn't know how it happened.

It's the most terrible thing in the world, to feel you've hurt someone. I was so upset, I could not even call the police or anything. I just trembled. I texted Mark, "I'm in trouble." Another car stopped and they called the police.

Then a wonderful thing happened: Somebody from the Sarasota Bay Club passed me and he called the staff and told them I was in the middle of the street. They sent someone to be with me, who moved my car and got me inside with the air conditioning on. By then the ambulance and police had come. Luckily the man really wasn't hurt; he had been on a bike that ran into the back of my car. I called our wonderful CEO, Gail Chase, to report how helpful the SBC staff were sending John, a concierge to help me.

Gail told me that the same thing had happened to her, and suggested that it might have been a scam. But scam or not, I was part of a scene with a man lying in the middle of the street.

When I told my son I thought I should stop driving, he said, "No, Mom; you didn't even get a ticket. Maybe you just need to be a little more mindful."

This shows the importance of sharing what you're really going through. And then you can focus on the part you can still control. I have a strong need for agency and control, and my kids enhance that.

Not all of my friends are so fortunate. One said to me, "I told my daughter I went out to dinner and she's furious; how could I dare go into a restaurant during the pandemic?"

The daughter of another friend told me that she thought he really shouldn't travel anymore. I said, "Look: Your father is in his late 80s, he's got good sense. He'll figure it out. Unless he is really in terrible shape mentally and has no judgment at all, let him exercise his own judgment."

The gradual change in the power dynamic with one's adult children is just another example of the transitions I've been studying all my life. Transitions are the links connecting me over the years from a teenager to someone now designated as part of the "old-old" demographic.

My particular transitions into old age started with voluntary retirement and geographical moving, followed by a struggle to find my place in a non-working world, followed by caregiving, then widowhood, and finally starting a new life.

This period of life is full of surprises. I am so fortunate to have Richard and his wonderful family—Andrea and Larry and Pamela and Greg—in my life. Having a romantic relationship at this age is such a wonderful surprise.

Another surprise: new friends. I have made wonderful friends at the Bay Club, many on my floor but others as well. Because I lived in a retirement community, during the pandemic I was able to have a social life. We had dinner parties, watched movies together and generally provided mutual support and, most important, fun.

This past month I was interviewed for a story that appeared in the Washington Post. I was also interviewed by a New York

CEO Senior Friendship Center Erin McLeod

Times reporter and a Wall Street Journal reporter. These are also surprising – that at my age my work has relevance. And I get emails every week from students all over the world thanking me for my work. The fact that my work is helpful to others, especially doctoral students, makes all the difference.

When the New York Times reporter asked me about how the pandemic has affected older people, I said I thought it should be viewed as a major non-event for many of them. Milestones that they expected didn't happen – the wedding that didn't take place, the trips, the visits with children and grandchildren, meeting new people.

Probably the most important strategy is reframing. It's not like other non-events that will never happen; they could occur at some time. You don't know at the time whether it's going to be delayed or forever. If it's forever, you have to come to terms with it. That's where I get into a piece of the dream: Is there a new goal? Is there a new way of looking at things?

I have done a lot of recent work on this subject with a support group I co-lead with retired lawyer Michael Karp, called the Aging Rebels, part of the Senior Friendship Center, led by my wonderful friend Erin McCloud. Since the lockdown began, we started meeting weekly online instead of in-person, discussing issues of loneliness, resilience and happiness. I also kept up my professional connections online during the pandemic, zooming with counselors in Australia to talk about the transition of becoming a new parent; with a group of women judges about issues connected with their upcoming retirements; and with library patrons in Cambridge, Massachusetts, about looking

The Aging Rebels

at the pandemic through the transition lens. I am still active with the Cosmos Club – an intellectual Club that has been an important part of my life since I was one of the first women elected to membership in 1988, and enjoy the interesting women who are part of the IWF (International Women's Forum). Most important has been the support and friendship from my book club members, first started in 2000 by Mickey Knox, Aina Segal, Gail Levin, Ina Schnell, Dorothy Firestone and later included Willa Bernhard, Judy Oxenhandler, Margo Evans, Cindy Malcolm, Sarah Pappas, Marian Peters, Michele Wolk, and Kathy Olrich. Our outdoor monthly meetings, even during the pandemic, were lifesavers.

Granted, this life is not a total bowl of cherries. Since having Covid I realize my health, though still good, is not what it was. I developed a "stiff heart." I always thought I had a warm heart, so I was shocked to hear that. I also had a vascular procedure to deal with a serious clot in my leg. And dental issues keep cropping up. And my mobility is not what I'd like. I worry that my future will be downhill and I don't want to live without quality of life.

But my children and their families, my friends, my work, are buffers and help me maintain perspective.

When Steve was dying I needed a therapist and luckily was referred to Paul White. I liked and admired him immediately. He is a "grown-up" and helps me maintain perspective.

Certain things on my bucket list will never happen. I always wanted to go to the Galapagos Islands. I talked about it for my 90th birthday, but my kids thought it would be too challenging for me. At this point I know I couldn't make the trip.

You really do give up certain dreams that you had. Some of them just don't make sense to you anymore, so it's easy to let them go. Others are more painful. Sometimes you have to grieve for a loss, and know that it's going to change the shape of your life. But with some things, you can reframe your situation and figure out something else that can make you happy – what I call a piece of the dream.

That leads to the ultimate question—what have I learned over these years? It turns out to be pretty simple: the keys to happiness include loving relationships, productive work, and living in a community. Right now I have that. I believe my good fortune is a result of good genes, love, attitude, and lots of good luck.

Yet there are always new surprises. Last weekend I was very busy with lunches, ballet, dinner with Richard and friends, a Sunday brunch, dinner Sunday night with our usual gang – Susan and Irving Fink, Lucia Blinn and Richard. Later that night my throat tightened up. I could not swallow. I took Emergence C, gargled and went to bed happy that I had taken care of it.

In the middle of the night I woke up feeling horrible, and was out of it the next day. On Tuesday I tested positive for Covid – *again*. I was immediately quarantined and everyone I had seen was quarantined and tested.

For me the horrible part was being isolated for at least 10 days. I barely managed the next two days trying to take care of myself, eat and drink. As usual my son Mark was on top of things and Karen was on the phone for emotional support. And of course, Richard, who luckily tested negative, was there on the phone. However, no one was helping me manage since no one was allowed in. I was worried about Richard's exposure because he had recently been diagnosed with congestive heart failure.

I began whining to Richard that I was unable to care for myself. He contacted his daughter Andrea and she found a wonderful nurse, Nicole, who helped me shower and changed my bed. But then she left and I was alone again.

Finally, on Day 3 – with endless whining and wishing I were an introvert instead of a full-blown extrovert – while figuring out how to get some soup heated I told myself I had to get a hold of this situation. I had to regain control.

So here is what I did: I knew human contact was essential so I asked Mark to arrange for Nicole to come in for two hours in the morning as I got myself together and to return at dinnertime to organize my dinners. Then I decided to figure out a routine. I would work at my desk taking care of the details of living in the mornings, arrange for a call from a different friend each day at lunch, read a book in the afternoon and watch Netflix at night.

Once I figured out a survival strategy I felt relieved and energized.

I cannot underestimate the support of the staff at Sarasota Bay Club, and my friends and family. As I think about at my 4 S's: My Situation and Supports are very strong. My Self sometimes gets a little wobbly but my coping Strategies are creative as long as I focus on using coping Strategies that pump up my natural optimism. So today my 4 S's are all good and I know I will survive whatever comes along.

I am a little afraid of the future – not of dying but of no longer being relevant or able to make a difference. Will I live too long? Will I continue to find purposeful activities where I feel I matter and am helping others? If I am alone will I be able to handle that loneliness? Will I continue to be resilient?

The answer came from a man I met when we first moved to Sarasota. He invited me to speak to his retirement community. After the speech and lunch we went to his tiny room with a small microwave and clothes hung on a portable unit.

I asked him directly, "Phil, how do you deal with your past when you were a celebrity, and today when you are not?" His answer: "It's simple. Wherever you are in life, you can make a difference. Today, I am limited in many ways. But as I sat and looked out my window, I saw staff members jumping over the hedge to get to lunch at the building across the way. I even saw a staff member trip and fall. I asked for an appointment with the community CEO, and suggested that a path be cut so the workers could easily get to lunch. When this was done, I realized it was small compared to things I had done in my earlier life. But I also realized you can still make a difference, no matter when."

I hope I can remember that, and continue to look at the future as a time of surprises and new adventures.

PART II

Selected Columns

Selected Columns About Transitions

THE FOLLOWING SELECTED COLUMNS appeared in the magazine *Better Living*, a *Sarasota Herald Magazine*, now out of print. I was hired to write monthly columns on different transitions with a focus on ways to handle them. I hope they are of interest and help to you.

✐✐

Mirror Mirror on the Wall: Our Love/Hate Feelings About Aging

Nancy K. Kchlossberg
Better Living 2012

I have been part of a group that is trying to establish a national Institute which we are tentatively calling the Institute of the Ages. Some community leaders have commented that people don't want to be part of something that suggests aging. That led me to conclude that age bias is alive and well. There are two aspects of age bias. The first is our own bias about aging—the messages we give ourselves, the assumptions we have about aging. The second are the messages we receive from society at large.

I will start with my own age bias. At a party, a convertible with the top down arrived. My first thought was how nice to be going to a party with younger people. I soon realized that the driver was a man who lives at the retirement community, Plymouth Harbor, with others in the car from the same place. I was startled. Is that the image I have of an 85-year-old man and if he is so "with it" why is he in Plymouth Harbor? My thought process reflected my bias about aging–that if you are in a retirement community you would not be in a convertible— especially in the back seat. I was doing what we do all the time—we categorize people by age. We categorize teen-agers, middle agers, baby boomers and older people. But you and I know the reality—that there is more heterogeneity as people age, not less.

Nancy Perry Graham, an editor of *AARP The Magazine* wrote in the January 2010 issue: "Just listen to the late-night comics. Scarcely an evening goes by that David Letterman… doesn't mock a certain 73-year-old politician with lines such as 'During the presidential campaign, Sarah [Palin] had to cut up John McCain's meat for him.' Recently Jimmy Fallon (granted, a youngster, at 35) announced that the family of a 70-year-old man who had run his 163rd marathon would celebrate by 'taking him out to a five-star emergency room.'" Similarly, many birthday cards for those over fifty have negative comments about aging like, "It's all downhill after 40." These cards and comics are merely the tip of the iceberg. We are bombarded with messages that older people have less—less energy, less opportunities, less sex, less money. Except for wrinkles it is all about less. Nancy Signorielli, Professor in the Communication Department at the University of Delaware, studied the under-representation of elderly characters on prime-time network. She concluded that "Television celebrates youth while it neglects and negates the elderly…and [while] television's messages about young adulthood are particularly vibrant and interesting, messages about middle and old age present a very different scenario because there are so few vibrant and interesting role models."

These negative messages about aging have reached all of us – that is part of the reason we are frantically pursuing the fountain of youth. Even though there has been a decrease in the number of people having plastic surgery, there are still millions of women and men who go in for tucks and hair dying in an attempt to look younger. When will we honor the person who says, "You look great–your hair is white, and your wrinkles sparkle?" When will we exchange wrinkles for wisdom, when will the messages from the media start honoring age? Changing attitudes means we must confront our own biases and celebrate rather than negate our age and wrinkles.

><

Navigating Life's Many Changes

Nancy K. Schlossberg
Better Living

The balancing act goes on all through life: with small children, you try and balance work and family; with aging parents, it's work, leisure and family; if you suffer from chronic illness, you're weighing your health needs with the needs of others.

In my work on coping with transitions, I found that success and potential for happiness depends on our ability to balance our positive resources and our deficits. If our positive resources outweigh our negatives, we are able to cope more effectively. It's important to remember: It is never one thing that ensures success; it is a combination—it is the balance.

For example, when Ruth Lee's husband presented her with the prospect of retiring to Florida from Connecticut, she was paralyzed with fear. "I cried until my mascara dripped onto my clothing and my children worried that I was having a teeny weeny nervous breakdown...I was crying at the idea of retirement...I wondered what I would do all day...I had worked on a newspaper...not exactly *The New York Times*... but...it was intoxicating. For the next 14 years I thought I was a combination of Maureen Dowd and everybody who wrote for the style sections of the *Times*...[and now I found myself] more in God's waiting room than in paradise. As for me, an abject failure in what a friend called 'retirement skills' a dropout from bridge, canasta, mah jong and golf, I wondered what I would do all day.

But several years later, Ruth Lee feels satisfied with the life she has created. "I sit on the terrace and watch the pelicans and I enjoy watching my husband enjoying," she says. "I have started painting and my work is regularly shown in art shows. I still write occasional articles for the paper."

So how did Ruth Lee turn what she viewed as a catastrophe that would compromise her identity and her sense of purpose into something positive? She strengthened herself by talking to friends and sharing her concerns with her husband; she developed coping strategies and networked with galleries in her new Florida community; she made many new friends and found a community of like-minded people; she developed a new purpose by finding outlets for her creative endeavors as an artist—and her identity is intact. As she says, "I didn't die in Florida."

Here are some tips that can help you balance your life so that your resources are strong as you navigate transitions.

Step I. Identify your potential resources or deficits.

These are clustered into four major categories, what I call the **4 S's: Situation, Self, Supports, Strategies**.

- **Situation**: What's going on in your life at the time of change?
- **Self:** What are your inner resources? What are you personal strengths—things you do well that help you deal with change? For example, are you optimistic, resilient, and able to deal with ambiguity?

- **Supports:** What people and activities can you count on for support during your transition?

- **Strategies:** Are you able to use a variety of coping strategies? What actions can you take to steer your transition?

Step 2 Apply the 4S System to your transition

People often ask, "Should I change careers?" "Should I move to a new city when I retire?" There is no easy answer to these and other questions about transitions. However, one can look at the 4 S's and ask: Is my Situation good at this time? Do I bring a resilient Self to the move? Do I have lots of coping Strategies in my repertoire? If all S's are positive, a move might be a good decision. However, if your Situation is problematic, your Supports minimal, you might want to delay the decision until you have built up supports in the new community and your Situation improves.

Step 3 Strengthen Your Resources

After you have identified which resources are working in your favor, you can strengthen those that are working against you. For example, there are books on imaging yourself thin. If imaging alone were the answer, I would be thin as a rail! I learned that it is not one factor like optimism, imaging, therapy that makes the difference—it is the balance of positives to negatives.

Even though we recognize that coping with transitions takes time, we see that people differ in how they cope with what seems to be the same transition, and often cope well with one transition but feel ineffective in the next. The difference is their balance of coping resources. When things do not go well, it is often because there are many more deficits than strengths.

And remember, the operative word is "time." Transitions take time. If you allow time to grieve over the things that you will miss from your previous life and give yourself time to recognize that things will come together as you start working on "getting a life," you will have a good shot at happiness.

Hopefully the 4 S system will take some of the mystery—if not the pain—out of change.

⌒⌒⌒

Aging with Panache—Mikhail Baryshnikov Shows the Way

Nancy K. Schlossberg
Psychology Today Blog, 2010

I watched Mikhail Baryshnikov dance at the 2010 Ringling Museum International Festival. He came onto a plain stage with nothing but a screen. Then he started dancing to a video of a young man dancing. And the young man was Baryshnikov at a much earlier age. He danced to his younger self. You saw three dancers—the younger, the older and the shadow. Now 62, he no longer leaps in the air but he still creates thrilling performances. He has style!

How does that relate to the rest of us? How do we continue to keep living a life where we feel we matter when our bodies are not what they once were? The answer: Let your creativity take the lead. The late Gene Cohen, an international expert on aging, director of the Center on Aging, Health, and Humanities at George Washington University, and author of *The Creative Age* and *The Mature Mind: The Positive Power of the Aging Brain,* found that the brain works differently as people age. In fact, older individuals are able to use both sides of the brain together, giving them an advantage. Cohen's research on the brain demonstrates that new brain cells continue to grow IF people are active participants in life. Dr. Cohen wrote, "I think that after 50 there's a new senior moment—a creative moment."

We do not have to fear diminished capabilities. We give up something; we take up something else. Baryshnikov announced at the Festival that he will no longer dance but I predict that he will continue to choreograph, and stay involved with dance. Each one of us can inventory our strengths and limitations, continue what we want, slow down the pace if necessary, but not give up.

One woman took up professional ballroom dance after she retired. She traveled around the country with her partner, participating in dance contests. At eighty she broke her ankle and realized her dance career was over and claimed, "I plan to reinvent myself." She became a volunteer fundraiser for several non-profits. A retired investigative reporter no longer writes several stories a week. He paces himself and writes a bi-monthly column. And I can no longer jog and use the stair master, but I can do water aerobics. We don't need to hide our limitations  but we do need to seek new opportunities, new possibilities. I help plan a Winter Forum on Aging for a non-profit in Sarasota, SCOPE, which we call, "A Lifetime of Possibilities." And that is what aging with panache is all about—figuring out your own lifetime of possibilities.

Overcoming Loneliness

Nancy K. Schlossberg
Better Living Magazine
March 2016; October 2018

A woman's support group selected loneliness as the topic for one of their monthly discussions. The leader of the session described her own experience of forty years ago after she and her husband decided to get a divorce. She felt lonely, empty, distraught. She read all she could find on the topic—at that time there was little on the shelves of bookstores and computers were not part of her life.

We all experience joy, excitement, misery, anger, love, longings, loneliness, happiness. You can feel one way today, one way tomorrow. It reminds me of the Disney picture "Inside Out" where a young girl experiences many emotions as she deals with her parents' move to a new community. Clearly moving evokes feelings of loneliness and loss. Her emotions of Joy, Anger, Disgust, Fear and Sadness are represented by cartoon figures. There is constant interplay of these emotions as Joy tries to get to the control center so she can control the young girls negative emotions and return her to joy. In a way, that represents what many feel as they age. As one older woman said, "I get excited about new ventures, irrelevant when I feel my voice is no longer heard, fear when I think about the future, especially loneliness and death. Most of the time the control center moderates the extremes."

The fact that people are living longer partially explains *AARP The Magazine's* conclusion that we are in the midst of a loneliness epidemic. According to a recent survey of their members,"35 percent are chronically lonely...compared with 20 percent...a decade ago." Robert Putnam, Harvard professor and author of *Bowling Alone*, attributes the epidemic to the decline of civic engagement. Brad Edmonson's article, "All the Lonely People" (*AARP The Magazine*, November/December 2010) reviewed the data, concluding that loneliness is "an equal opportunity affliction," unfortunately one that can compromise one's health. According to John T. Cacioppo, director of the Center for Cognitive and Social Neuroscience at the University of Chicago, "Loneliness has surprisingly broad and profound health effects...There is mounting evidence that loneliness significantly increases the chances of diabetes, sleep disorders, and other potentially life-threatening problems." (quoted in Brad Edmondson's AARP article).

Even though we recognize the enormous toll loneliness takes, it was not until I read Robert Weiss's book, *Loneliness: The Experience of Emotional and Social Isolation* (MIT press, 1973) that I was able to understand my own and others experiences. Weiss identifies two different forms of loneliness both resulting from what he labels "relational deficit" (p. 18). The first, loneliness of emotional isolation, arises when an intimate relationship is interrupted by death or other problems. I can relate to that. When my husband died after 50 years of marriage I felt bereft. The second kind is loneliness that results from social isolation—a break in one's social network. I can also relate to that. For example: For years, I felt very much part of the community largely because I was an active player in a new start up. I felt that I mattered to the community. Unfortunately, the start up failed. For a period of time, I lost my social network.

Caregivers are particularly at risk for loneliness. One man described his emotional isolation. His wife does not appreciate what he does and becomes angry at him. Another caregiver expressed social isolation when he said, "There's another piece that no one's talked about. It's the loss of friends. We've all experienced it, people that you shared things with aren't there anymore. You wonder if they're afraid, is it because they're embarrassed, uncomfortable or don't know how to handle it?

The circle of every day social friends is shrinking. They don't ask to have coffee anymore."

Other at risk groups includes returning veterans, new widows and widowers, newly retired and newcomers to a community. Anyone who looses an intimate relationship and/or a social network of friends is at risk. Those who are married or are part of a group can also feel marginal and unhappy. If a marriage is unsatisfactory, but before one declares it is time to end it, one can feel very isolated.

I asked a retired therapist, widowed for about 6 years, to describe her loneliness experiences. She responded, "It is part of the human condition...Yes, I am lonely. It is a theme of my life. I came to America as a teenager and have always felt like odd man out. I stand on the outside. That means loneliness is ever present."

We can all point to our own experiences or that of others and identify loneliness. But the more important question is what, if anything, can you do about it?

Strategies for Overcoming Loneliness

1. Study the topic. The leader of the womens' group who talked about her loneliness resulting from divorce, said the first thing she did was to read everything she could on the subject. At that time (mid sixties) she found only one book which she underlined and studied.

2. Focus on Emotional Isolation. So you have lost your most intimate connection. Take time to grieve. Join a grief group. Talk about it with a therapist. Over time start looking for a new attachment figure. Let others know you are looking. More and more people of all ages are going on line to meet someone special.

3. Focus on Social Isolation. One woman, recently widowed but lonely for several years as she took care

of a spouse with Parkinson's, joined a temple. The Rabbi and membership welcomed her. She has become very active and is totally absorbed with contributing and benefiting from being part of this community. Identify an organization and offer to volunteer. Become engaged.

4. Start Networking. Malcolm Gladwell underscores the importance of connecting through "strong ties" where you would find jobs or dates through personal connections and through "weak ties" with people you barely know. Both are critical, but if you are only using "strong ties" you probably already know the same people. It is through "weak ties" that you meet people and groups you did not previously know (see *The Tipping Point: How Little Things Can Make a Difference*, pp. 54,55).

In Conclusion: Just remember, Rome was not built in a day but if you have the goal of developing a full life, it might take time. We all need a confident and a social network.

><

Even Happy Transitions Can Be Bewildering—But Why?

Nancy K. Schlossberg
Better Living Magazine
July 25, 2013

Why do happy transitions—like a wished-for job or relationship—upset us? I interviewed a new college president about her transition. She was thrilled to be selected but wondered why she felt depressed after starting the new job. A newly married couple moved into their first home. Following the excitement hanging pictures and showing off their new home to family and friends, they felt letdown. Why do transitions-even ones we elect-upset us so?

In the thirty years since I started studying transitions, I have learned some things I can share. First, there is the expectation that the new home, the new car, the new baby, the new job will make us content and joyful. Often reality is not quite what we imagined or hoped for. It's about expectations.

Second, and, more important, every transition changes our lives. Transitions change our role, relationships, routines, and assumptions. For example, your new home or your new job changes your role. You are now a homeowner; you are now a college president; you are now an account executive; you are now a licensed plumber. With each new role change, you are in touch with new people and new colleagues—new relationships. And with each transition your routines change. If you change jobs, clearly where you go for coffee changes; if you move, where you take your clothes to be cleaned changes. And last, your assumptions about the world can change.

Retirement-which is a career change-is a perfect example of the challenge of change. When you were working, your roles, relationships, routines and assumptions were in order. When you leave that life, it takes time until you establish a new set of roles, relationships, routines and assumptions. The same is true when you experience any transition—divorce, return to school, job change, and so on.

So, even with a desired change there is disruption in your life. Until you establish a new life—or get a new life—you will feel bewildered.

The answer: Be prepared and be patient. Be prepared that following a new transition there might be a let down. Be patient as it takes time to get a new life.

Celebrate The New Year, Celebate Your Failures

Nancy K. Schlossberg
Better Living Magazine
January 2014

I was nominated to be on the national board of a major organization. The application was very challenging. Secretly I knew I would get appointed. When I received the letter informing me that I was not selected, I felt very disappointed and like a failure. But was I really a failure?

As I think about celebrating the new year, I think about celebrating what we can learn from what we label our failures and challenge our often-erroneous belief that we are failures.

Erma Bombeck provides a context for this discussion when she wrote, "Failing is what most of us do...but we have still managed to go on breathing...I have several reactions when I hear people introduce me [with]...accolades...so glowing that I don't even recognize myself. I figure Mother Teresa just flew in...I would like to propose a new wrinkle to introductions. Instead of listing a speaker's successes, why not list the failures? Born average, our guest tonight never rose above it...Her first and last comedy album...raced to oblivion...She has never won a Pulitzer Prize...never been interviewed by Barbara Walters... (*Washington Post* July 30, 1991, p. B8)" And none of us would consider Erma Bombeck a failure.

Another example: Ten women, who received Woman of Distinction awards from the National Association of Women in Education, described how they achieved their dreams. They identified perseverance, commitment, and goal setting as key factors. On a different note, the final speaker, me, said, "I want to speak about the failures each of us had had. We would not be standing before you if we had not faced failure. Remember that successes have more failures than failures have."

So, if failing is something we all do, something we are all accomplished at, why fight it, why deny it? It is not failing that is the issue but how we define it, cope with it and grow from it. The following strategies might help put failure in perspective

1. Use failure to your advantage. Retired Gen. Stanley McChrystal was forced to resign for inappropriate remarks he made that were critical of the White House. Did he fade away and die? No. In fact, he lectures in a course on leadership at Yale University called "Coping with Failure." Mark, a senior in high school threw the loosing pass in the final football game. Devastated, he thought he could not go on. However, when it came to writing his essay for college admission, he wrote a dramatic story about his loosing pass and how it has made him a "better" person. He used his failure to get into college.

2. Reframe and redefine failure. Don't catastrophize. Realize that failing in one arena doesn't mean you are a failure. Individuals tend to generalize. It is too easy to label yourself a failure. Dr Joachim Stoeber and Dr Dirk Janssen in a paper, "Anxiety, Stress & Coping" suggest that the key is reframing what one calls failure in a more positive way; for example, by focusing on what has been achieved, rather than on what has not been achieved. 'It's no use ruminating about small failures and setbacks and drag yourself further down,' he said. 'Instead it is more helpful to try to accept what happened, look for positive aspects and—if it is a small thing—have a laugh about it.'

3. Read books about others' experience. Carole Hyatt and Linda Gottlieb, after each failed at a job, decided to

write a book on the topic, *When Smart People Fail*. The authors' concluded, "There is no such thing as failure. Failure is the judgment of an event: the way you see loss of a job, the closing of a play." They interviewed hundreds of people who had been fired or experienced a failing career or marriage. Talk to anyone, and there is a story about failure.

4. Review your coping options. There was a cartoon about Snoopy being depressed because the employee of the month award was given to someone else. Snoopy could become depressed and begin thinking that he (I checked it out—Snoopy is a male) was a failure or he could ask himself:

- Can I change the award and make it mine? The answer is no. It is a fact and Snoopy cannot change that award.

- Can I change the way I look at this situation? Clearly, yes. Snoopy can see this as a wake up call-a chance to get more training, to develop new skills, to do what is necessary to turn the situation around.

- Can I relax as I deal with what I initially defined as a failure? Yes. Snoopy can begin meditating, walking, swimming-anything to reduce the stress level accompanying not achieving success.

- So, whenever we are faced with a challenge we can ask ourselves three questions: Can I change what is happening? If not, can I change the way I see it? And can I reduce my stress?

In conclusion, some schools focus on helping young people learn character attributes as well as academic skills. The headline of story in *The New York Times Magazine* "Why our kids' success-and happiness-may depend less on perfect performance than on learning how to deal with failure" highlights the importance of embracing and celebrating failure (September 18, 2011).

Back to my New Years resolution. I resolve not to be freighted of failure but to welcome it, learn from it and move on.

❧❧

Repairing Broken Relationships

Nancy K. Schlossberg
Better Living Magazine
December 2014

Many songs reflect the heartache that comes with a broken love, an ending career, a ruptured friendship. We memorialize endings, we romanticize new beginnings, but often we handle them poorly.

A few examples follow:

- Bill has been living with a woman for several years. She has ended their relationship and insisted they live apart. He cannot end it. He just waits and hopes that she will have him back.

- Natalie was a widow-in-waiting for several years, knowing her husband would die, but not knowing when. Even though she was prepared, she is having difficulty trying to carve a new life.

- Ted resigned from his job as CEO of an organization he founded. His identity was interchangeable with the organization's. He has begun to feel regret, ambivalence, unsure about what he did but more important where he will go.

- Molly and her son have not talked in years. She reported that he was the one who broke away. At one point he told his mother that he was angry because he felt total lack of acceptance from her when she discovered that he was gay.

- Ralph, a high-ranking army officer, told me he hated his parents for what they did to him as a little boy. He described one incident—a time when they locked him out of the house. In fact, he did not go to his father's funeral—that is how angry he still was. He never let go of his anger.

- Martha, a sixty-year-old woman, talked about the horrific fight she had with her husband. She threatened suicide and felt they could never repair their relationship.

- Meridith and Ebony were best friends. Meredith found a romantic partner. There was a period of adjustment where the two women saw less of each other since clearly romances take time. Ebony felt left out and hurt. On the one hand, she was happy for her friend; on the other she felt slighted.

Any broken relationship—between two people, or a person and an institution—begins with the ending, followed by continuous reevaluation, and finally with the decision to repair it or just walk away and stay away. Figuring out what to do about a ruptured or broken relationship—that is the question. As you decide on your course of action, here are some pointers to consider:

1. **Take time to grieve.** Broken relationships are transitions—the more invested you are in the relationship the more difficult the transition. These relationships evoke complicated reactions. You are dealing with the event—the breakup. You are also

dealing with what you had expected and is not occurring. For example, a mother and daughter have stopped talking. That is a major event. But they are also dealing with a non-event—the celebrations not shared.

2. **Develop a leave taking ritual.** We have all dealt with ending something that was important to us. Confusion and ambivalence precede the actual decision to stay or not to stay. Sara Lawrence-Lightfoot points out the importance of handling exits well and our lack of leave taking rituals in her book *Exit: The Endings that Set us Free.* The Peace Corps is a perfect example. Much time is spent orienting new recruits but much less time helping volunteers adjust as they return to their own societies. In other words, attention must be paid to the leave taking process.

3. **Learn about Collaborative Divorce,** a new procedure gaining traction, developed to help people work out a harmonious way to end the relationship while keeping lines of communication open and agreed upon. See the following link to an article describing the process. *http://www.thinkadvisor.com/2014/08/25/ collaborative-divorce-a-win-win-dissolution* Rather than just 2 lawyers, the parties hire a team—the lawyers lawyer, 1 accountant, or 1 financial planner as a neutral and mental health professionals for additional support. Together with their team they look at the entire picture with the goal of resolving the conflict peacefully and reaching a durable mutually acceptable agreement.

4. **Consider forgiveness.** Why, asked Cora, should I forgive? After all, what he did was unforgiveable. Answer: Forgiveness is not about the perpetrator of harm. It is about you. It is about freeing yourself from hatred, from angry feelings, from being hurt.

Robert D. Enright argues that forgiveness is so important. He offers a process that will help the forgiver. (*Forgiveness is a Choice: A Step-by-Step Process for Resolving Anger and Restoring Hope*, American Psychological Association, Washington, DC 20001).

Enright points out that forgiveness does not deny that we have been hurt. We have a right to feel hurt, angry, or resentful (Pp. 24). Forgiveness is not condoning or excusing, forgetting, or justifying.

The following case is an instance of forgiving and actually forgetting. A young woman, Wanda, described her adolescence. She hated to bring friends home in case her mother was drunk. Her mother embarrassed her and made her feel ashamed. She remembered one night when her mother chased her around the kitchen with a knife. Years later, the young woman expressed how grateful she was. If her mother had been less volatile she might have stayed in her hometown. This way, she moved away and developed her own identity. She also forgave her mother when her mother was very ill and for medical reasons had to stop drinking. She began to understand the cause of her alcoholism and to forgive her. Wanda is free and remembers her mother with love and appreciates all the things her mother had done for her—ice skating together in the park, joint art lessons, shopping for fun clothes. Over time Wanda was able to see the total picture and put the negatives in perspective.

5. **Explore Reconciliation.** It is certainly possible to forgive but not reconcile. But realize that one of the options in repairing a broken relationship is to "bury the hatchet," get back together and negotiate a new phase in the relationship. Reconciliation is often difficult to achieve because most relationships have patterns, habits and comfort zones. Clearly, reconciliation will force new patterns. It is a new relationship with an old connection.

The bottom line: You have a choice. To live filled with anger at another or to move on, let go of the anger, forgive, maybe even reconcile. It is almost 2015. Do any of us want to go into the New Year without reexamining our relationships? Living your adult life estranged from someone who was once central to your existence can be debilitating. Forgiving is freeing. It is the beginning of a new year.

❧

Creating Your Own Ritual

Nancy K. Schlossberg
Better Living Magazine
September 2015

As fall and winter approach, we celebrate Labor Day, End of Romadan, Rosh Hashanah, Yom Kippur, Sukkoth, Simchat Torah, Halloween, Veterans Day, Thanksgiving, Hanukkah, Christmas, Kwanzaa and many others. Each holiday includes rituals that are central to the celebration. These rituals, according to the late Anthropologist, Barbara Myerhoff, help us celebrate transitions and mark the "inevitable facts of human experience" that "punctuate and clarify" critical times in our own lives like birth, marriage, and death.

But what about the ordinary transitions we all experience that have no rituals attached to them? Some examples include moving to a new city, moving to a retirement community, not getting the promotion you expected, starting menopause, sending your last child off to college, the death of your best friend, the death of your dog. These, and many others, are transitions with no accepted rituals. And that, according to Myeroff, is the problem and lends itself to the solution—designing your own secular ritual.

Francesca Gino and Michael I. Norton found that those who participated in a ritual acknowledging a loss were better able to handle and manage their grief. ("Why Rituals Work" in *Scientific American,* May 14, 2013). For example: after a breakup the person who was left took pictures of the two of them, cut up the picture and burnt them in the park where they first kissed.

A personal example: I will never forget the morning our daughter, Karen a high school senior, came bursting into our bedroom to announce that she had decided to go to work, move into her own apartment and not attend college. Shocked, I screamed: "We will discuss this later."

Coincidentally, that very morning, I was on my way to hear a speech by Barbara Myerhoff who discussed how rituals can help people deal with "marginal periods"—when they are shifting from one phase of life to another. As she described the many significant events and nonevents that we fail to ritualize she used the case of eighteen-year-olds moving out of their parental home. I could not believe that she talked about what I was experiencing. I left the speech, called my husband immediately and said "Don't get angry with Karen. I know how we need to handle this."

Based on her speech, we decided to ritualize Karen's departure by giving a celebration dinner and inviting our closest family friends. We chose gifts and wrote poems to commemorate her past and celebrate her future. We promised to pay for phone installation, which would connect Karen to her past—but expected her to pay the monthly phone charges, connecting her to her future. And that is the point of a ritual to acknowledge that you are leaving one part of your life but have not quite moved to the next phase.

Similarly, Ms. Magazine reported a homemade ritual that acknowledged a young woman's non-event—not finding Mr. Right. When she realized time was passing, her parents sent out a notice to their friends announcing that their daughter was ceasing to look for "Mr. Right" and place settings were available at Macy's.

Rituals can also help make sense of senseless things. A woman I know lost her father in the Vietnam War. He is Missing In Action. She discussed the pain of not ever knowing. She keeps hoping and wondering. To promote healing and offer support two veterans started "Run For The Wall." They motorcycle across the country once a year to draw attention to those not accounted for. This ritual has grown. The woman whose father is lost finds this group ritual comforting and she looks forward to it. Meyeroff talks about the importance of group activity, in this case group solidarity.

Develop Your Own Ritual

Here is how one family developed a personal, secular ritual.

Older people agonize over the decision to stay in place or move to a retirement community. One woman expressed the dilemma when she said, "I am moving with mixed emotions. I keep going backwards, then forward. This might be the most difficult transition I have faced." The in between period that Myeroff describes applies to many older people—seeing yourself as independent and "young" at the same time realizing that you are seen as old. A man, age 89, considering a move said, "I am not ready yet." His partner, age 86, replied, "If we are not ready at 86 and 89, when will we be ready?"

When they finally decided to move from their beautiful apartment to the retirement community, they developed a ritual to ease the transition. They were "betwixt and between" their old life and their new life. Following Myeroff's suggestions, they decided to have a July 4th party to say goodbye to their old apartment and announce moving to a smaller apartment in a nearby community. Their ritual followed the guidelines Myeroff suggests: an activity shared with others, an opportunity to name the confusion, a chance to receive solace from others as they rehearse for the future. The group talked about the transition and toasted the old and new apartments with champagne.

And In Conclusion

Rituals help you deal with who you were and who you are becoming. They are particularly helpful when you are betwixt and between. According to Myeroff, "rituals punctuate and clarify that otherwise amorphous condition." "People facing situations that induce anxiety typically take comfort in engaging in preparatory activities, inducing a feeling of being back in control and reducing uncertainty" (*Scientific American*, May 14, 2013).

>[·]~·<

Senior Romance: Does Saturday Night Have to be the Loniest Night in the Week?

Natalie, a widow, is worried about being lonely on Valentine's Day. "I'm in my seventies, attractive, enthusiastic, fun. I had a really happy marriage and want to find a man with whom to share my life while I am still healthy. I'm not sure how to proceed. The casserole brigade won't work for me—I don't cook."

Natalie represents a growing number of people living longer than ever before. According to the U.S. Census Bureau, "During the 20th century, the number of persons in the United States under age 65 has tripled...and the number aged 65 or over has jumped by a factor of 11." And those over 85 are the fasted growing group. In addition, women outnumber men 5 to 2 after age 85. That led one woman to tell her ailing husband, "You have to fight to stay alive. You are demographically irreplaceable."

The fact that people are living longer partially explains *AARP The Magazine's* conclusion that we are in the midst of a loneliness epidemic. According to a recent survey of their members,"35 percent are chronically lonely...compared with 20 percent...a decade ago." Robert Putnam, Harvard professor and author of *Bowling Alone*, attributes the epidemic to the decline of civic engagement. One antidote to loneliness is to become involved in community activities, volunteering, or learning. You can identify such opportunities by linking to The Gulfcoast Community Foundation's web site, *Youdbeperfectforthis.org*. For others, romance is how they wish to alleviate loneliness.

How are Seniors Looking for Romance?

Our stereotypes of aging men and women often include shuffleboard, TV watching, and early bird specials, but not a lot of first dates, romance, or sexual encounters. However, it is important to note that coupling in your later years is on the rise. Deborah Todd, a reporter for the Pittsburgh Post-Gazette, found evidence that you are "Never Too Old." "Seniors... are looking for companionship, and many are looking for a partner to spend the rest of their life with" (May 29, 2012, p. A-7). It could be about a meaningful connection, which often includes sex or physical intimacy. It could be about comfort and security, a close friendship, even marriage. But whatever the particular outcome, the importance of having a special relationship beyond close friends and family is important for many. AARP's study, "Lifestyles, Dating and Romance: A Study of Midlife Singles," pinpoints some gender differences: women want companionship and men want companionship and sex.

Mary Ann, a widow, was perfectly content working, volunteering, and coordinating a widows group in her over-55 community. She retired gradually spending time more and more time visiting children and grandchildren. Like so many new widows and widowers, the last thing she was looking for was another serious relationship. Mary Ann kept in touch with a friend who had introduced her to her late husband. Last October that friend invited her to Hilton Head for a six-day visit. Her friend did not mention that she had also invited a widower, John, and another couple. Soon after the vacation, John called Mary Ann to confess, "I'm too old to waste time, so if you're interested, I would love to see you again." They arranged for John to visit from a neighboring state. Mary Ann described how nervous she was. To try and hide her anxiety she kept jumping up and down, getting things from the kitchen, and taking walks. The weekend was followed by many more as they developed a nice friendship. She reports, "I felt I could trust him, and we both shared similar values. He would kiss me on the cheek, with an occasional hug. The turning point came several months later when we were both invited to a party. That night he gave me a romantic kiss. I have not had feelings like this since I was a teenager." Mary Ann was not looking for romance but is absolutely thrilled to have found "true love" at her stage of life. The relationship escalated; they became engaged on May 23 and married on November 3rd.

Mary Ann met through a close friend. What about all those having trouble meeting others? How do they do it? How can they strategize to increase their chances of connecting?

Now for the $65,000 question: How do older people make connections?

The bottom line is that people meet in all kinds of expected and unexpected ways. They meet through shared activities, at the checkout counter of a grocery store, in an elevator, at a political event, a dinner party, in a retirement community, through friends, on facebook and even online. One woman who met someone her daughter worked with, exclaimed, "I never expected to meet someone special and certainly did not think my daughter would be my matchmaker!" (See the link to some dating tips *http://www.findaqualityman.com*)

No matter how you meet, it usually involves networking. Bestselling author and writer, Malcolm Gladwell underscores the importance of connecting through "strong ties" where you would find jobs (or dates) through personal connections and through "weak ties" with people you barely know. Both are critical, but if you are only using "strong ties" you probably already know the same people. It is through "weak ties" that you meet people and groups you did not previously know (see *The Tipping Point: How Little Things Can Make a Difference, pp. 54,55*).

Some Examples

Bonnie and Bob knew each other though they were both married to other people. Then they each lost their spouses within the same year. And coincidentally, Bonnie had just moved into the retirement community where Bob and his wife had lived. Before long, they started eating dinner together. Bob wanted to get serious. Bonnie wasn't as sure. As time went on, Bonnie became equally committed. She feels very lucky. "All we do is play," she explains. "I feel like a teenager all over again." Bob adds, "When my wife died, I felt so alone." These days, neither of them feels alone any longer.

Alice met a man while waiting in the lottery line at the grocery store. She and a man started flirting. "Want to go halfsies if one of us wins?" she asked. When she actually won $11, they split it and went to Starbuck's for coffee. They discovered they lived two blocks from each other, and both had owned horses. They exchanged phone numbers. She called him and they went to the Italian movie, "Do We Have a Pope?" They held hands and she loved it. Then when they drove home, he kissed her and gave her a full-body hug. She told herself, "Oh my God, I am not ready for this." And she has not seen him since.

For those who have not met either by chance or intention, many agree it is time to go online. Many, but by no means all, older people have reservations about the Internet. As one woman, who chose to remain anonymous, said, "Going online has a negative connotation. It implies that you could not get someone on your own. And you really don't know the background of those you are meeting."

Leah finally succumbed to her friend's encouragement and registered with J Date. She thinks it is amusing—how people present themselves in unrealistic ways. Short people say they are tall, fat people underestimate their weight. There is a great deal of exaggeration. She bucked the trend and told the truth about her age and weight on her profile. She wrote she likes to travel first class. She received many messages from thirty year olds thinking she was rich and would take care of them. Such is the problem with being so honest!

Despite her reservations, she met someone of a reasonable age who, she said, "looked stylish." A great fit! She arranged to meet him in a bar; one of her friends went to the same bar to be there, just for security. They met, got along. He would like it for life but she is happy as it is. They see each other exclusively.

Another Internet example: Molly, age 90 and Ed, aged 82 met online. Molly said, "I knew a knight on a white horse would not come and sweep me off my feet. I knew if I wanted something to happen, I'd have to do something about it." She, therefore, applied to *match.com* even though she felt foolish doing so. It worked. Ed answered her ad and found they both love scotch and Shakespeare. The link to the interview with Molly and Ed shows romance, enthusiasm, and happiness. *http://blog.match. com/2011/11/16/molly-and-ed-love-is-still-in-the-air-at-90-and-82/*

Whether you meet through "strong" or "weak ties" some issues emerge.

The Elephants in the Room

<u>Sex</u> is clearly the number one elephant in the room. One 82-year-old man exclaimed that he is now a sex object—women are coming onto him all the time. Mel, a 70-year-old widower, explained that one barrier to his dating, especially younger women, is that he can't always perform sexually because of health issues. His wife understood but if any other women entered his life down the road, it would be a potential stumbling block.

Amy, a woman in her seventies, sees a man exclusively whom she met through shared political activities. They have no intention of living together and they agreed to forego sex. They like their platonic relationship.

In general, men worry about being impotent and women worry about how their bodies look undressed. Many women agree that sex would have to be in total darkness—at least at the beginning. One woman expressed a different point of view. "I feel more at home with my body now than when I was younger and large breasted women were idealized. So perhaps I won't undress in the dark."

<u>Childrens' reactions</u> can be another elephant in the room. Mark became agitated when he realized his mother was dating. He was worried someone would take advantage of her, give her bad advice, or even scam her. He knew of a case where the mother of his friend started dating, met a man, married him and then found out that "he was a scoundrel." She divorced and put her wedding ring back on so men would assume she was married. She is absolutely through with men and dating.

Children are afraid that money will be given to the new person or that the parents would not have as much time for them or their grandchildren. Whatever the fears, adult children can interfere with their parents' romantic lives. One man felt that the delay in his relationship proceeding smoothly was the childrens' protectiveness of their mother. Another man felt that part of the reason for his breakup was the adult childrens' need for their mother's attention—financially and emotionally.

On the other hand, many children are delighted that their parent has found someone. It relieves them of worry and makes them happy.

The Takeaway

There are some things that connect all ages—the need to matter to someone else, the need to love and be loved, the need to be appreciated. To make this happen, it is necessary to identify your connectors—those people you know with whom you can discuss your interest in meeting someone else. Then consider how you will access people you do not know, possibly through social media. Every contact does not end in immediate success. Sometimes it takes contacting two or three connectors. It is a "what's next" strategy that can work. So don't let Valentine's Day be the loneliest day of your life and Saturday the loneliest night in the week.

Back to Natalie who has made a decision to be proactive. She has identified what she wants, and is strategizing how to get it. She plans to talk to all her friends—her strong connectors—and if that does not work, she will go online or hire a matchmaking service. We will revisit Natalie next year and track what has happened. Her current mantra—don't give up!

><del></del><

Create Your Own Happiness—"Accentuate the Positive, Eliminate the Negative"

Hard to believe but true: according to George Vaillant, Presidents Kennedy, Eisenhower and Roosevelt "suffered illnesses that would have merited a 100 percent disability from the Veterans Administration." Clearly, [attitude and] subjective health are as important to aging as objective physical health" (2002, p. 187). "Whether we live to a vigorous old age lies not so much in our stars or our genes as in ourselves" (p. 213).

Not surprising are the findings that those with a disability who maintained positive beliefs were more likely to make a recovery according to Yale epidemiology and psychology professor Becca Levy. "We think the results are very promising and encouraging and show that mindset may be associated with recovery in elderly patients" (This study appeared online in *The Journal of the American Medical Association*, Nov. 21).

We can observe many examples suggesting that attitude and well-being are linked. For example, an 87-year-old woman who has endured many tragedies including the death of one of her 4 children from a brain tumor, death of her husband of 60 years, murder of her brother is starting a new chapter of her life. Her children put her online and she met someone new and is now focusing on the future.

An 80-year-man who is legally blind, took two subways and one train to visit his granddaughter in the hospital. I commented on his ability to do what would seem impossible for most of us. He said "I made up my mind NOT to be a tragic figure; I made up my mind to function as independently as I possibly could."

Another example: Canadian writer Alice Munro announced it was time for her to retire from writing. She had lost her husband and now was ending a long, successful career. She made a conscious decision—to become more social by accepting more invitations. "I do things quite purposefully now to get out on the surface of life" (Charles McGrath, "Putting Down Her Pen to Let the World In" *New York Times*, July 2, 2013, p. CI).

These survivors made up their minds to flourish. They do not know it, but they are part of the Positive Aging movement that fosters resilience while focusing on one's strengths and happiness. Hundreds of books, articles and conferences on the topic reflect the degree to which the movement has traction. A just-published article from the Harvard Medical School called *Living to 100: What's the secret?* concludes that "if you bring to your life appreciation and respect, and embrace aging with good humor, grace, vigor, and flexibility, you will—at the very least—be happy to grow old." The subtitle of the report says it all: "Positive Psychology: Harnessing the power of happiness, mindfulness, and inner strength," The conclusion—a sunny outlook might protect the heart and brain" (p. 8).

A friend read a draft of this column and suggested that I was overlooking the difficulty many have as they try to adopt a positive outlook on life. I agree with her—it is difficult, but not impossible. A few tips about ways to adopt a sunny attitude follow:

Tip 1. Give yourself a pat on the back for making the effort to adopt a positive attitude. Remember that you need to 1) commit to doing it and 2) take whatever steps are necessary—whether it is physical therapy, counseling, taking courses, etc.—or to increase your needed skills. My own situation is a case in point. During the last year of my husband's life, he had care around the clock. As he was dying, I had emergency back surgery, followed by a hip replacement and two months in a rehab nursing facility. Despite what seemed to me overwhelming challenges, I made up my mind that I would walk again and I committed to a rigorous course of physical therapy.

Tip 2. Challenge your thinking. Martin Seligman, one of the founders of the Positive Aging movement and a psychologist who studies the effect optimism has on well-being, suggests that you need to argue with yourself when negative thoughts creep in.

Tip 3. Compare yourself with others in even more challenging situations. When my sister-in-law was dying of Lou Gering's disease, she kept telling me it could be worse. She compared herself with those in worse shape who had to be fed with a feeding tube.

Tip 4. Be on the lookout for resources such as books and conferences about successful aging. The Institute for the Ages located in Sarasota, Florida is hosting this year's conference on Positive Aging. These conferences provide opportunities to learn how to be more positive and build on your strengths.

Tip 5. Remember to repeat Johnny Mercer's advice "You've got to accentuate the positive."

You've got to accentuate the positive

Eliminate the negative

Latch on to the affirmative

Don't mess with Mister In-Between

You've got to spread joy up to the maximum

Bring gloom down to the minimum

Have faith or pandemonium

Liable to walk upon the scene

To illustrate his last remark

Jonah in the whale, Noah in the ark

What did they do

Just when everything looked so dark

Man, they said we better, accentuate the positive

Eliminate the negative

Latch on to the affirmative

Don't mess with Mister In-Between

～～

Why Mattering Matters

By Nancy K. Schlossberg

Jim, a retired policeman, had great difficulty adjusting to retirement.

"The day I turned in my gun and badge, I lost my identity, my work relationships, and my sense of purpose. I no longer mattered," he lamented.

And Roberta, a retired homemaker (I call homemakers CEOs of small family businesses.), claimed, "My children needed and depended upon me. They're gone and I feel disjointed."

Hal, a retired CFO of a Fortune 100 company, felt that now that he was "old and retired" his life was "hollow."

That cry—"I no longer matter"—is echoed over and over as people struggle to deal with aging and retirement. Think of Willy Lowman, the protagonist in Arthur Miller's play "Death of a Salesman." His desire "to excel, to win out over anonymity and meaninglessness, to love and...be loved, and above all... to count." When he roared out, "I am not a dime a dozen! I am Willy Lowman..." he was expressing this desperate need for significance.

The late distinguished sociologist from the University of Maryland, Morris Rosenberg, used the word "mattering" to describe the need we all have to believe "that we count in others' lives, loom large in their thoughts, make a difference to them." When you feel that you matter, you feel sought after, appreciated and depended upon. Rosenberg identified mattering as an overlooked motive—one that explains performance, behavior, even well-being.

Mattering to oneself, to others and the world is the coordinating, although not single, issue that guides our understanding of ourselves: Do I know who I am? Do I appreciate myself? Do I feel competent? Are my inside and outside worlds congruent? Do others appreciate me? Do I feel needed? Rosenberg argues that mattering is a universal, lifelong issue that connects us all.

Many older people and many retirees complain of feeling marginalized, not noticed, no longer players. You can have money and jewels, but if you feel sidelined, out of the loop, you will be unhappy. If your voice is heard, you will feel happy.

But what is mattering? There are five ingredients.

1. Attention. Professor Emeritus Robert S. Weiss wrote, "When I attend a professional conference, I tend to feel marginal."

2. Importance. Columnist David Brooks wrote, "Let me tell you what men want…They want to feel important and part of something important."

3. Appreciation. Reflected in the sentiment, "I volunteer for a local organization. I feel that my work is appreciated."

4. Dependence. "I volunteer for Meals on Wheels. The people I serve depend on me. It makes me feel good."

5. Pride. "Family and friends are proud of how I am handling life."

Rosenberg studied the effects of not mattering on homeless individuals in the Washington, D.C., area and delinquent boys. With graduate students at the University of Maryland, where I was a professor of counseling, I took his work and applied it to adult learners and retirees. We found that those institutions of higher education with practices, programs and policies that were responsive to the needs of adults, had a higher percentage of adults completing their programs—and who were therefore happy. Rosenberg suggested, and I found, that retirees who feel appreciated report feeling happy.

The first step is to understand the dimensions of mattering.

The next step is to figure out what we can do to make others feel they matter and what we can do to help ourselves feel we matter. First, an example of making people feel they matter.

I attended a meeting honoring the volunteers of the Sarasota Jewish Family & Childrens' Service. Rose Chapman, the CEO of the organization, thanked the retirees for all that they do. But she went much further than that. She invited all the retirees to call her, to stop by, to visit with her. She expressed an interest in getting to know each one of them. The group responded positively; they felt they mattered to her and the organization.

To ensure your own happiness, here is A Mattering Recipe—A Way for You to feel You Matter:

- Get involved, stay involved. Volunteer. Work part time. Get out there and become essential to a group or an organization.

- Harness the power of invitation. Take advantage of invitations. You never know where they will lead.

- Make others feel they matter. Show your appreciation for what others have done and make that appreciation public.

- Develop a purpose—something that matters to you. Mattering has two sides to it: You need to feel you matter and you also need to figure out what matters to you. But that is the topic of a future column. Does this recipe guarantee total bliss? No, but it is a start.

PART III

Summary of Transition Theory

Summary of Transition Theory

IAEVG-NCDA SYMPOSIUM

TRANSITIONS: THEORY AND APPLICATION

Nancy K. Schlossberg

Invited Specialist for "Career Theory in an International Perspective"

Professor Emerita, University of Maryland

Former President of the National Career Development Association

Co-President, TransitionWorks

**This article was written in 2004 but updated in 2022

Abstract

How do people negotiate the ups and downs of living? What differentiates why people facing a similar transition handle it so differently? To answer these questions, I conducted studies of people in transition, including geographical moving, adult learners returning to school, men and women whose jobs were eliminated, clerical workers dealing with work/family balance, retirement, as well as non-events like not getting promoted, not having a baby, and not having the career or relationship you expected. This paper describes the model highlighting several ways in which it has been applied in real life situations.

The Transition Model

Everyone uses the term transition. It is, therefore, important to remember that no transition is exactly like another. They can be categorized in the following ways:

- Anticipated transitions: the major life events we usually expect to be part of adult life, such as marrying, becoming a parent, starting a first job, retiring;

- Unanticipated transitions: the often-disruptive events that occur unexpectedly, such as major surgery, a serious car accident or illness, a surprise promotion or factory closing;

- Non-event transitions: the expected events that fail to occur such as not getting married, being unable to afford to retire, or not getting promoted.

To summarize: Transitions are events or non-events, anticipated or unexpected that alter our lives in significant ways. To better understand the complexity of transitions, three major components will be described.

Component 1: Transitions change one's roles, relationships, routines and assumptions

Transitions alter our lives—**our roles, relationships, routines, and assumptions**. Transitions such as the birth of a first child or taking early retirement appear to have little in common, but both adjustments change a person's life. For example, becoming a new parent adds a role, changes relationships with one's spouse or partner, clearly changes one's routines, and changes one's assumptions about self and life. The same is true when one retires. One's role as worker disappears, relationships with former co-workers change, daily routines are altered, and assumptions about oneself change. It is not the transition per se that is critical, but how much it changes one's roles, relationships, routines, and assumptions.

The bigger the change, the greater the potential impact and the longer it may take to incorporate the transition and move on.

Component 2: The Transition Process Takes Time

Transitions take time, and people's reactions to them change—for better or worse. At first, people are consumed by their new role such as being a new graduate, a new widow, an unemployed worker, a recent retiree. Gradually, they begin to separate from the past and move toward the new role, for a while teetering between the two. I interviewed a man who retired six months ago from the public school system. He said his first month was very difficult as he was so used to his routine, his relationships, and his professional identity. But now, six months later, he is very comfortable with his new set of activities. He is very active in an exercise program, serves a volunteer for the court system as a guardian ad litem, and is participating with the League of Women Voters.

The process of leaving one set of roles, relationships, routines, and assumptions and establishing new ones takes time. For some the process happens easily and quickly, for others it might take years. There are many people floundering, looking for the right niche.

Component 3: The 4 S System for Coping with Transitions

Even though we recognize that coping with transitions takes time, we see that people differ in how they cope with what seems to be the same transition, and often cope well with one transition but feel ineffective dealing with the next one. How then do we handle this journey, live through it and learn from it?

Identifying the features common to all transition events and non-events, however dissimilar they appear, takes some of the mystery out of change. These features are the potential resources or deficits one brings to each transition. They can be clustered into the following four major categories, what I call the 4 S's:

Situation. This refers to the person's situation at the time of transition. Are there other stresses? For example, if one retires and one's significant other becomes critically ill, coping with retirement becomes difficult. If one is offered a major promotion at the time when one's teenagers are in trouble and one's parent is moving into a nursing home, the Situation is extremely stressful.

Self. This refers to the person's inner strength for coping with one's transition. Is the person optimistic, resilient, and able to deal with ambiguity? Clearly one's personality, and style of behaving influences how one copes.

Supports. The support one receives or that is available at the time of transition is critical to one's sense of well-being. If a new retiree, for example, moves to a new city knowing no one, with no supports, the adaptation might be slowed down. If a new mother is single, with no support system, this too can be extremely challenging.

Strategies. There is no magic coping strategy. Rather, the person who uses lots of strategies flexibly will be better able to cope. For example, a person who handles transitions just by talking to others may be better served by utilizing more coping strategies including exercising, gathering information, brainstorming, or joining a support group. According to Leonard Pearlin and Carmi Schooler (1978) people cope by using multiple strategies. These can be grouped into those that try to change the situation, those that help reframe the situation, and those that help manage one's emotional reactions to the situation.

How does the 4 S system work? Take the question retirees often ask, "Should we move to California when we retire?" There is no easy answer to that. However, one can look at one's

4 S's and ask: Is my Situation good at this time? Do I bring a resilient **Self** to the move? What kind of Support can I count on in the new community? Do I have lots of coping Strategies in my repertoire? If all S's are positive, a move might be a good decision. However, if one's Situation is problematic, one's Supports minimal, there might be a decision to delay the move until one builds Supports in the new community and one's Situation improves.

To restate: The Transition Model clarifies the transitions we are experiencing by identifying:

- The degree to which one's life has been altered (changes in roles, relationships, routines, assumptions);

- Where one is in the transition process (considering a change, beginning the change, two years after the change); and

- The resources one can apply in making it a success (each of us approaches the transitions with a unique set of resources).

Applications

The transition model can be used as a framework for conducting research on any group or person in transition, a guideline for developing interventions with individuals, groups, and organizations. The model provides the cognitive framework so that counselors, coaches and others can listen to clients, help them assess their resources for dealing with change, and identify ways to strengthen their resources. Selected examples of ways in which transition theory has been used illustrate its utility.

The Transition Guide—A Research and a Counseling Tool

The Transition Guide, designed as a self-scoring instrument, enables individuals to asses their resources for coping with change (Schlossberg and Kay, 2003). The Guide consists of 56 questions. Answers to these questions result in a profile of each individual's strengths and deficits.

Two questions from each section of the Guide illustrate this (Note: Scores range from 1-5):

- Your Situation: How You See The Transition

  Looking ahead, I feel able to—

  _Plan ahead with great difficulty

  _Plan ahead with great ease

  I see my situation as—

  _Totally out of personal control

  _Totally within personal control

- Your Self: Who You Are

  I usually face life as—

  _A pessimist

  _An Optimist

  I feel a sense of control or mastery as I face transitions—

  _Never

  _Always

- Your Supports: What Help You Have From Others

  Can I count on support from my family?

  _Inadequate support

  _Fully adequate support

  Can I count on support from my friends?

  _Inadequate support

  _Fully adequate support

- Your Strategies: How You Cope

  I cope by—

  _Using few strategies

  _Using a range of strategies

  I cope by—

  _Not using transition knowledge

  _Applying knowledge of the transition process

The Guide itself is a vehicle for self understanding. For example, it (or some modification of it) has been used in studies of rural women, returning learners, retired government employees. It has been used to help employees deal with work transitions.

The Guide was used by an international organization as a training tool with staff from Asia. Participants completed an on-line version and discussed each section of the Guide with other participants and the leader.

A Textbook—Counseling Adults in Transition

A textbook, <u>Counseling Adults in Transition: Linking Schlossberg's Theory with Practice in a Diverse World</u> (Anderson, Goodman, Schlossberg, 2012; 2022), now in its fifth edition, can be used by professional and paraprofessional counselors, social workers, and psychologists with their clients. It presents adult development theories as a background for what helpers need to know, then details the transition framework and applies it to individual transitions, relationship transitions, and work transitions.

Trade Books

Five trade books translate different aspects of transition theory for the general public. *Overwhelmed, Coping with Life's Ups and Downs* (Schlossberg, 2nd edition be Taylor in 2008) presents an overview of transition theory written for adults who are not professionals; another (Schlossberg and Robinson, Simon & Schuster, 1996) *Going to Plan B* and now out of print, examines non-event transitions—those events you expected to happen that did not-and how they change your life with suggestions about how to cope; another (Chickering and Schlossberg, 1995) is written for college students showing them different strategies for coping with college as they move into, through, and out of the educational system; and two self-help books by Schlossberg, *Retire Smart, Retire Happy: Finding Your True Path*

(Schlossberg, 2004, American Psychological Association) and *Revitalizing Retirement: Reshaping your Identity, Relationships and Purpose* (American Psychological Association, 2009) helps people examine their psychological portfolio necessary for a successful retirement; and *Too Young to be Old: Love, Learn, Work, and Play as you Age* (2017 chronicles transitions for people as they age, American Psychological Association).

Staff Training

The model can be used to train staff working with those in transition. For example, the transition of moving into an elder care facility—especially one in which residents can move to different levels of care—is a unique set of transitions. The Transition Model can be used as a way to train staff so that they might better assist the residents with these major changes. The goal would be to help residents discuss the transition, how they perceive it, and their resources for coping with the move.

Another example, instituted by The National Institute of Corrections, is the development of a program to train those who work effectively with offenders and ex-offenders. Jo Ann Bowlsbey, Barbara H. Suddarth, and David M. Reile, principals of The Career Development Leadership Alliance, Inc., developed an extensive training package consisting of eleven modules, which when successfully completed qualifies participants to apply for the Career Development Facilitator Certification through NBCC-CCE. Participants are prison counselors, caseworkers, local community college personnel who work with offenders or ex-offenders.

As part of the program Bowlsbey and colleagues utilized Transition Theory. Module 1 describes the theory; Module 10 illustrates how to apply to theory as one conducts a transition interview with an offender about to be released from prison.

As a way to teach Transition Theory they state the four assumptions of the theory (pp. 1-20): Life is characterized by change, transitions are events or non-events that cause change, transitions have varying effects on different people, and success in life is highly related to ability to cope. The training materials highlight the life-changing transitions associated with being incarcerated. All roles, routines, relationships, and assumptions of the offender and the offender's family are in flux.

To help trainees better understand the world of the incarcerated, trainees are asked to list typical events and non-events of offenders, and then show that each offender has a different set of resources—the 4 S's. Those being trained are asked to apply the model to several case studies. In addition, trainees are given a worksheet as a guide for conducting a transition interview. In a later module, trainees are asked to interview offenders and ex-offenders asking questions about their resources for coping—the 4 S system.

"This type of theory offers hope for offenders since it assumes that control over life and its roles can be gained by learning to cope in a rational, cognitive way (pp. 1-21)."

Application in Japan

Overwhelmed: Coping with Life's Ups and Downs was translated into Japanese and has been used with many career advisers who are part of Japan Career Development Association. Seven advisers were surveyed to uncover how they used the Transition model. Their verbatim comments are included in Appendix A. To summarize, they used the theory as the basis for teaching seminars, conducting workshops, giving lectures as well as counseling in person, and counseling through e-mail. Several specifically commented on the value of thinking about non-event transitions.

A few of the adviser's comments reflect the way they incorporated the theory into their work:

"The question most often asked is 'I have \
considering a career change but just can't take\
plunge and go for it. What should I do?"Draw\
from the Theory of Transitions, I usually ask them\
brainstorm by making a list of possible plans."

"I want [clients] to learn from sharing their stori__
of transition with others...I want them to see transitions
as opportunities."

"I talk about...Transition Theory at Career Workshop
I regularly conduct for new employees...I give each
group a pile of 30 cards featuring possible events and
nonevents in their corporate life...After this activity,
I give them an extensive lecture of Transition Theory,
introducing the concept of the four S's."

"Mr. A...came to see me at an outplacement company
[where] I work as career consultant...In helping Mr. A's
exploration, I introduced the concept of the four S's and
encouraged him to take stock of his resources to cope
with transition."

The Future

The model provides a systematic way to think about
transitions. It clearly will be modified as more data is collected.
In recent weeks, I have received e-mails from doctoral students
studying a variety of transitions: retiring from professional
sports, rural women returning to school, adult learners
studying via the internet. These studies will expand, test, and
modify the theory.

References

Anderson, M.L., Goodman, J.,Schlossberg, N.K. (2022). *Counseling Adults in Transition: Linking Schlossberg's Theory With Practice in a Diverse World.* (5th edition). Springer Publishing.

Chickering, A. W. & Schlossberg, N. K. (1995). *Getting the Most Out of College.* (2nd. ed.). Columbus, OH: Prentice Hall.

Harris, J., Suddarth, B. H. & Reile, D. M. (n.d.). *Manual and Participant Manual for the Offender Workforce Development Specialist Training and Certification*. This material was written under contract with the National Institute of Corrections (a part of the U.S. Department of Justice) by the Career Development Leadership Alliance, Inc.

Mizuno, M. (November 8, 2003, February 1, 2004). E-mail correspondence.

Pearlin, L.I., & Schooler, C. (1978). Social sources of emotional distress. In R. Simmons (Ed.), *Research in community and mental health* (Vol. 1, pp. 217-248). Greenwidh, CT: JAI Press.

Schlossberg, N. K. & Kay, S. (2003). *The Transition Guide: A New Way to Think About Change*. Potomac, MD: TransitionWorks, Inc.

Schlossberg, N. K., Waters, E. B. & Goodman, J. (1995). *Counseling Adults in Transition*, (2nd ed.). New York: Springer Publishing Company.

Schlossberg, N. K. (1989). *Overwhelmed: Coping With Life's Ups and Downs*. Lanham, MD: Lexington Press.

Schlossberg, N. K. & Robinson, S. P. (1996). *Going to Plan B: How You Can Cope, Regroup, and Start Your Life on a New Path*. New York: Simon & Schuster, A Fireside Book.

Schlossberg, N. K. (2004). *Retire Smart, Retire Happy: Finding Your True Path*. Washington, DC: American Psychological Association, Life Tools.

Schlossberg, N.K. (2009). *Revitalizing Retirement: Reshaping your Identity, Relationships and Purpose*. Washington, DC: American Psychological Association, Life Tools.

Schlossberg, N.K. (2017). *Too Young to be Old: Love, Learn, Work, and Play as you Age*. Washington, D.C. American Psychological Association, Life Tools.